Small Town Bound

**Your Guide to Small-Town Living,
from determining if life in the slower lane is for you,
to choosing the perfect place to set roots,
to making your dreams come true**

By
John Clayton

Small Town Bound

Your Guide to Small-Town Living,
from determining if life in the slower lane is for you,
to choosing the perfect place to set roots,
to making your dreams come true

By
John Clayton

CAREER PRESS
3 Tice Road
P.O. Box 687
Franklin Lakes, NJ 07417
1-800-CAREER-1
201-848-0310 (NJ and outside U.S.)
FAX: 201-848-1727

SMALL TOWN BOUND
ISBN 1-56414-251-5, $11.99
Cover design by Foster & Foster
Cover illustration by Ruth Moses
Printed in the U.S.A. by Book-mart Press

To order this title by mail, please include price as noted above, $2.50 handling per order, and $1.00 for each book ordered. Send to: Career Press, Inc., 3 Tice Road, P.O. Box 687, Franklin Lakes, NJ 07417.

Or call toll-free 1-800-CAREER-1 (NJ and Canada: 201-848-0310) to order using VISA or MasterCard, or for further information on books from Career Press.

Library of Congress Cataloging-in-Publication Data

Clayton, John, 1964-
    Small town bound : your guide to small-town living, from
determining if life in the slower lane is for you, to choosing the
perfect place to set roots, to making your dreams come true / by
John Clayton.
       p. cm.
    Includes index.
    ISBN 1-56414-251-5 (pbk.)
    1. Urban-rural migration--United States. 2. Cities and towns-
-United States. 3. Country life--United States. 4. Quality of
life--United States. I. Title.
HT381.C53 1996
307.76'2'0973--dc20   96-21270
                                                            CIP

Acknowledgements

Many thanks go to the people whose comments and stories are sprinkled through this book, who freely volunteered to share their experiences and lessons.

I owe a gigantic debt to the people of my town, who showed and taught me a great deal. Much of what's collected here originated with them. To protect their privacy, these friends and their town go unnamed in this book.

Additionally, I received invaluable guidance and encouragement from the following people around the country: John Ware, Luther Propst, Paul & Jacklyn Clayton, Mary Keller, Julie Yao, Lisa Easton, Jim Howe and Jim Murtaugh.

Contents

Chapter 2
Evaluating a small town
Which *small town is right for me?*

So you want to move to a small town?

It might be the scenery that draws you—mountains, rivers, farmlands or forests. It might be images of a rural lifestyle or the accessibility of recreational opportunities. It might be a job opportunity for you or your spouse. It might be memories of a tight-knit community you experienced as a child. Or it might be visions of a place free of crime, traffic or stress.

Whatever planted this seed, whatever nurtured it, you've arrived at a notion you can't shake. You want to move to a small town. Maybe you've even chosen one. Perhaps friends or family live there. Maybe the area's economy is growing, it placed highly in a rating guide or you recently visited and realized you never wanted to leave.

Still, the thought of such a radical change is scary. Abandoning your metropolitan area, with friends, cultural opportunities, a lifestyle to which you've grown accustomed. What can you expect from your new home? Will the cultural adjustment be too hard? How will the natives accept you? What can make the process easier?

Let this book be your guide.

A new migratory trend

You are not alone. A decades-long trend of rural depopulation—people leaving the farms to seek better opportunities in the cities—is reversing itself. According to the U.S. Census Bureau, the population of rural areas grew 4.7 percent in the 1980s. Many small towns, particularly those located in scenic areas, are now facing development pressures. These towns used to wonder how to plug the drain of young people moving out; now they wonder how to accommodate the overflow of people moving in.

Everything about this migration is new, not just the direction. In fact, if you're part of it, you're part of one of the hottest demographic trends in the country. In analyzing the trend, sociologists have pointed out two unique factors. The first is motivation. In the past, people moved from rural areas to cities to improve their economic or cultural opportunities. Or they moved from one metropolitan area to another (often seeking neighborhoods resembling those they left) because of the demands of a career. But today, people are moving away from the cities for a host of other, interconnected reasons. These reasons are frequently summed up using the phrase "quality of life." We'll examine these reasons and their relationships throughout the book.

The second unique factor is the demographic diversity of the new migrants. It used to be that young people left rural areas to start life in the city. But the faces of migration are changing. For example, many of the people now moving to small towns are retirees, freed of obligations to a career. Towns in the south and southwest, blessed with warm weather, have been particularly popular retirement destinations. However, many senior citizens are discovering that the quality of life they seek involves more than weather: a range of leisure-time opportunities, amenities such as clean air and water, and the sociability and friendliness of a small town.

Another type of small-town migrant has similar motives but a very different lifestyle. The much-celebrated "modem cowboy" is a professional whose use of modern technology allows him or her to locate anywhere in the country. These people are broadening the economic and cultural horizons of formerly remote areas, with exciting implications for the future of rural America.

Beyond these telecommuters lies a whole range of migrants—blue-collar workers, retailers, entrepreneurs and employees of companies that have decided to move their entire operations to rural communities.

Whichever of these classes of migrants you fit in (or even if you're in a class by yourself), you'll face the same types of adjustments. Because, let's face it, small towns are different. No matter how embedded they are in the national psyche, no matter how much we think of them as "typically American," small towns have a culture very different from that of metropolitan areas. In some ways, moving to a small town is like moving to a foreign country.

It doesn't feel like a foreign country, of course (and luckily!). People there speak English, drive on the right-hand side of the road and vote in Presidential elections. Compared to your old neighbors, these people really are different. Living in a small town makes them that way. If they were born and raised there, they were indoctrinated into this unique culture at an early age. If they moved there from elsewhere, they likely adapted their personalities to fit their new surroundings. Or they chose these surroundings to fit their unique personalities. Their viewpoints, prejudices and perspectives on a variety of issues may catch you by surprise. And a slip-up may be costly. Despite the best of intentions, your statements or actions (or failures to act) may send the wrong message, and you'll find yourself disliked or resented.

Unless you have this book. Consider this book your "cultural guide" to the small town. Just as you might read a book on Japanese culture before taking a trip to Japan (or moving to Japan or doing business with Japan), read this book before moving to a small town. And refer to it once you're there. Use it to understand the motives and desires of the people you encounter.

An important step is to understand the traditions and folkways—the mindset—of the people who will be your new neighbors. Once you do this, you'll be better able to bridge a cultural gap—a vital step in setting up your new life. You may even decide, with this new knowledge, that small-town culture isn't really for you.

The next step—adopting this culture as your own—is up to you. You may decide to dive in, impressed with how it works for others. Or you may respect it in others but reject it for your own lifestyle, retaining your old traditions and values in your home (much like Americans living abroad, who celebrate Thanksgiving on a day that their neighbors find no different from any other). With either decision, however, knowledge of that culture—of those rules and ideals that everyone around you is following—will be essential for your happiness and success in your new home.

What is a small town?

Ask five people to define a small town, and you'll probably get five different answers. (Ask the Census Bureau to define a small town, and it'll refuse to answer: a population of 25,000 constitutes a "city," it says, and 2,500 to 25,000 is a "place," but a small town has no official definition.) To one of the seven million residents of New York City, a population of 100,000 residents may constitute a small town. On the other hand, Wyomingites see Cheyenne, with a population of 50,008, as not just a city but a metropolis.

Some urbanites use the terms "small town" and "country" interchangeably. Either is simply a place with fewer people than the city or its suburbs. On the other hand, some people make an important distinction. A "small town" (the term "village" is frequently used in the Northeast) is a place with businesses, shops and residential neighborhoods. "The country" is simply farmland or forest or desert, perhaps with a residence every mile...or every 20 miles.

Nevertheless, when you think about moving to a small town, you're probably not thinking about a specific population figure. You're thinking about the benefits of a relative difference in population density, intangibles such as neighborliness, community or a perceived simplicity of life. This book uses the term "small town" in that sense—as a difficult-to-describe atmosphere, rather than a strictly defined product of population or architecture. Perhaps the best summation of this state of mind was offered by a resident of my town, trying to define the most valuable characteristic of our friendly, close-knit community, who said, "Only in a place like this can you have a conversation with a misdialed phone number."

It's a quality of life you seek, rather than a population figure. You may find that quality of life in a town with 50 people or 50,000; you may find it "downtown" or in a place where your nearest neighbor is seven miles up a dirt road. It depends on your personality and that of the surrounding community. Regardless of how you define the small town, it's far different from the city or suburb you're leaving.

You may be hesitant. How, you're thinking, can one book describe small towns all around the country? How can it cover that wide diversity: the Midwestern heartland, the desert oasis, the New England village, the Western cow town, the agricultural hamlet, the logging camp, the university community, the ski or golf or beach resort?

The answer is that it can't, fully. There's no question there are differences. One of the things we enjoy about many small towns is that they retain a great deal of regional and historical character. They're islands of individuality in an increasingly homogeneous society. So this should not be your only guide, especially if you are moving to a different region of the country. If, for example, you're moving from Boston or Nashua to a New England village, you may have some familiarity with what you're getting into. But if you're moving there from, say, San Antonio, you may want to learn about the wonderful peculiarities of New Englanders.

However, regardless of the particulars of your metropolitan origin and your small-town destination, your biggest challenge will be adjusting to the rhythms of the smaller community. We uniquely address those differences, as you'll soon read.

How to use this book

This book is structured to meet your needs, attempting to address the various issues that could arise in the process of your move. Chapter 1 addresses your decision about whether to move to a small town:

- It helps you identify your motives for considering this move and the implications of those motives.

- It paints a very generalized picture of small-town life, helping you evaluate the truthfulness of your images of the small town: safe, neighborly, gossipy, quaint.

- Finally, it spells out the tradeoffs involved in moving to a small town and how you can answer for yourself the question "Is this move right for me?"

Chapter 2 focuses on evaluating small towns, helping you choose the particular environment that will be right for you:

If you have no idea what town you might want to move to, this chapter tells you how to identify some possibilities.

- It presents some general rules of thumb to help you distinguish good small towns.
- It discusses a wealth of specific criteria against which you can judge your candidates.
- It also gives instructions on acquiring the information you need to make your decision.

In Chapter 3, we'll look at getting a job, which is often one of the most important considerations for potential migrants:

- Tips and techniques for getting a job before arriving in town.
- Factors to consider about working at home or for a small business.
- The differing attitudes toward employment held by many people in the small town.

Of course, if you decide to move, you've made only the first step. Chapter 4 covers how to start your new life in the small town:

- How to meet and form bonds with your new neighbors.
- How to enter the community in ways that will make you feel valued rather than resented.
- Factors you may need to consider in setting up your career.

Chapter 5 discusses prospering in your small town. Because (as you'll soon discover if you don't already know) small towns are usually lousy places to make money, your "prosperity" will be defined in other ways, such as:

- Dropping some old, ingrained habits that may put you at odds with the small-town philosophy.
- Some approaches to handling the rumor mill.
- The implications of the small town's priorities on community life over personal status.

Finally, Chapter 6 examines how to preserve your newfound quality of life, ensuring that you find the small town as fulfilling and promising 20 years from now as you do on moving day.

The Resources section in the Appendix suggests places to go for more information on various topics.

The book also contains three running features included as sidebars. First, throughout the book, we'll be listening to the advice of numerous individuals who have successfully made this move themselves. These individuals vary in age, gender, occupation, socioeconomic status and geographic location. Their experiences and recommendations illustrate various points through self-contained *profiles*. In these sidebars, you'll hear them tell their stories: how and why they decided to move or what they found when they did so.

A second series of sidebars analyzes how small-town life is depicted in the *media*. Does the current fervor for small places reflect reality or the romantic impulses of a Hollywood screenwriter? How might your affection for certain movies or television shows be played out in a real-life small town?

The third series of sidebars summarizes the recommendations of each chapter in a feature called *20 Questions*. Like the children's guessing game, these sets of questions should help you hone in on answers to issues such as which town to choose or how to get a job. Though the questions summarize points in the text, they should also provide new perspective by giving different twists to issues and mixing up the order of their presentation.

A warning: The book is filled with cautionary tales. It's filled with the difficulties of small-town life: the economic insecurity, the isolation, the rumor mill, the lack of amenities. That's not because the author hates small towns—indeed, I live in one, and moving here was one of the most productive, enriching, satisfying acts of my life.

On the other hand, I was lucky. I was suited to small-town life. For too many, however, the small town has not lived up to their dreams. They've had to move on, bitter about the experience, vowing that next time they'll look before they leap. The cautionary tales here are for the benefit of their contemporaries—people who are ready to leap and want to look first but (until now) haven't known how to do so.

Another reason this book doesn't play up the many benefits of small-town life is that these benefits are so widely known and appreciated. There's little need to sell you on the value of never being in a traffic jam (or of defining a "traffic jam" as two cars behind a stop sign). There's little need to introduce America to the joys of knowing and respecting your neighbors, feeling a closer link to nature and the environment or leaving your car unlocked on the street. These and other attributes of small-town life are rightfully part of our American heritage and our vision of a collective future. They're dreams many of us share, dreams to which you don't need an introduction.

What you need is a guide: Which aspects of these dreams can come true...and how.

Chapter 1

Deciding to move to a small town

Is a small town right for me?

Perhaps leaving the city is just a vague notion in your mind. Perhaps it's just an idle thought that surfaces when you're returning from a long weekend in the country, when you're cursing the traffic of your daily commute or when you or your loved ones are confronted with the ugly realities of urban crime.

So let's take some time to study this notion. In this chapter, we'll look at some of the motives for moving to a small town and how those motives can color some of the experiences you'll have there. We'll paint a portrait of small-town life—how your lifestyle might change if you were to make such a move. Finally, we'll give you some tools to help you evaluate whether your move will help you meet these objectives.

A. What do you want?

1. Motives and implications

Let's briefly suppose that the publishers of *Small Town Bound* are right this minute calling you on the phone, conducting a survey of the book's buyers. They want to know, in 20 words or less, why you want to move to a small town. What are you going to say?

Now let's suppose you've got Call Waiting, and on the other line is a close friend, surprised to learn that you bought this book. Your friend, too, wants to know why you want to move to a small town. Again, what are you going to say? If you haven't already, you might want to set down the book right now and formulate answers to these questions. They're different questions, of course: your friend knows more about you and will let you explain it in more than 20 words (probably even an hour, if you need that long). But the expanded and condensed versions will reveal different things, and you may find both exercises valuable in assessing your state of mind.

Here are four sample answers to our hypothetical survey of motives:

Jill: "I grew up in that town, and I want to get back to my roots."

Steve: "I've owned a second home there for years, and my work is such that my business won't be affected by the remote location."

Madeline: "I've decided that quality-of-life issues are more important than money."

Tony: "I want a safer environment to raise my family, even at the expense of career fulfillment for me."

All are valid and well-thought-out reasons. But the differences between them have important implications for these peoples' experiences after they move. Each motivation brings different advantages and disadvantages and suggests different areas where each person will want to focus attention.

For example, Jill probably knows people in town, so the social adjustment may be easier for her. Even if she doesn't actually know people in town anymore, she may be familiar with personality types she met while growing up there. On the other hand, her rosy view of life there may be colored by nostalgia—for example, as a child she didn't have to worry about making a living.

Steve's economic worries are minimal (assuming his business analysis was rational and reasonable, rather than clouded by emotions), though moving the business will probably demand a lot of his attention. The key to his happiness may be in trying to preserve that carefree "vacation" feeling now that his second home is cluttered up with his everyday lifestyle.

Madeline knows she'll have economic troubles, but she isn't going to worry about them. She can focus her attention on appreciating the town's lifestyle—meeting people, taking advantage of recreational opportunities and so forth. On the other hand, after a year or two with little money, she may end up reconsidering money's importance in her life.

Tony's focus on family will probably be a good fit with the small-town philosophy. Most kids are in fact better off with a more rural lifestyle. Which is not to say it's easy or foolproof: aimlessness, boredom, alcohol, drugs and violence among youth (and among adults, too) are major problems in many small towns. Tony may need to continue to make career and personal sacrifices to spend more time as a role model for his children.

As you look at your own motives, consider their implications. What will be your biggest challenges? Where will you want to focus your energies? What will be your rewards? How will you be able to measure your success?

2. Pushes and pulls

Do your motives have to do with qualities you are seeking or qualities you are *fleeing*?

Jot down some phrases describing your reasons for moving. How many times does the word no appear? For example: "No traffic. No crime. No noise. No beggars. No pollution. No ex-lovers who live nearby and keep walking past my house with a hangdog expression." These are "push" reasons, as compared to "pulls." They're reasons you want to get out of the city, but they don't say a lot about your destination. (Alabama? Wisconsin? Nevada? Anywhere could match.)

There's nothing inherently wrong with "pushes." Indeed, the fact that you're aggravated by traffic/crime/noise suggests that you are a better candidate for moving to a small town than your neighbor, who's not bothered by them. However—especially if your list contains more "pushes" than "pulls"—two refinements might be worthwhile.

The first refinement is to try to turn the pushes into pulls by getting rid of the word no. Instead of "no noise," say, "quiet." Instead of "no pollution," say, "good air and water quality." Adopting a positive attitude is always better for your state of mind; in this case, it also focuses your attention forward—on goals and dreams you want to pursue—rather than on your rearview mirror.

The second refinement is to add some "pulls" to the list. Yes, most small towns will meet your "push" criteria, but any town has unique attributes of its own. If you've never paused to consider which attributes are important to you, you may be setting yourself up for disappointment. Is weather important, and what kind of weather do you want? Age distribution? Ethnic diversity? Do you need access to a good golf course, ski area, lake or ocean? How far do you want to be from a hospital, airport, shopping mall or library?

If you were to say, "I hate being single, I want to get married," without identifying the qualities you value in a spouse, chances are you'd end up with a bad match. Your randomly chosen spouse might meet certain bare criteria (averting loneliness, perhaps, or helping you do the dishes), but the two of you wouldn't share interests, goals or dreams. Keep in mind that the range of small towns in the country—while not quite as great as the range of potential spouses—provides numerous options to match your personal desires and needs.

Of course, just identifying some "pulls" isn't enough. You'll also need to ensure before you move that your destination does in fact have those qualities. And you need to be realistic: you probably can't find mountains, oceans, a university and an airport all in one small town (unless you redefine Los Angeles as a small town). Which criteria are the *most important*? Once you've identified them, Chapter 2 will help you choose and evaluate small towns against your list.

As you evaluate your "push" reasons—reasons for leaving your city—you might come up with the following:

- Too much crime.
- Too much traffic.
- Too much pollution.
- High cost of living.
- I don't know my neighbors.
- Grumpy people.
- Not enough free time.
- There's no sense of community.
- The area has a cookie-cutter sameness.
- High taxes.
- Too much time spent commuting.
- Bitchy, greedy or manipulative people.

As noted, these are reasons to leave the city, but they don't necessarily tell you much about where you want to move. If you can turn them around to positive statements—ideally getting as specific as possible—you can start honing in on what you're looking for. For example:

- "Too much crime" could become "I want to be able to walk around my neighborhood at night."

- "The area has a cookie-cutter sameness" might become "I want to live in a neighborhood with interesting architecture, preferably Victorian."

- "Too much time spent commuting" could become "I want to live in a neighborhood that's less than five miles from my work place."

If you don't think the positive statements say all that much more about a destination, look again. By becoming more specific, this person has identified she wants to live in a neighborhood in town, rather than out in the country; that neighborhood should be comprised of older, established (Victorian) homes; and the neighborhood needs to be close to her job. She's picking the job first, so her choice of a small town will be largely determined by career considerations.

3. What's changing? You or your surroundings?

There's a question you should ask yourself before you move, and it's an uncomfortable one: Do you expect a geographic change to magically improve your personality?

In other words, are there personal problems or issues you hope this move will resolve? If so, are your expectations realistic? For example, let's say you're overweight, and you want to move to a small town because you expect to do less driving and more walking. Does your lack of exercise have to do with opportunities or your willpower? A more serious example: Perhaps you believe that moving to a small town will break a cycle of destructive behavior (e.g., relationships, alcohol, drugs or emotional disturbances). Again, is the move going to do it, or does most of the work have be done internally? Small towns do have a different philosophy, which you can harness constructively; but they also have temptations, and the temptations are more focused in the more confined environment. It'll take strength of character to avoid them.

This is not to say that you can't "be a better person" in a small town. My own case is proof of that: I was unhappy with a too-yuppified lifestyle in the city; I wanted to be more giving, more involved in community activities. My family asked the difficult question: "How is moving going to solve that? Why don't you work at changing yourself here, where you have more support?" I explained that a big part of my problem was that I was unable to relate to the big city. I didn't feel at home there. In a small town, I hoped to be better able to connect to the community and thus be better able to achieve my goals. Experience has (luckily!) proven that analysis correct.

The key, however, is that I knew I was a "small-town person." That's another important question you have to answer: "Does my personality match that of the small town I'm considering?" Ideally, this book will help you shape your response. But in the end, it's you (using what you know about yourself and your destination) who must come up with a difficult yes or no.

In sum, though moving to a small town can help you focus on personal struggles or your outlook on life, it can't substitute for your hard work in considering and evaluating these difficult issues.

4. What makes for happiness?

When you think of people who live in a small town, you probably think of them as well-adjusted, happy, healthy and productive. Most people do. A nationwide survey showed that Americans believe rural residents are in better health, more honest and more able to enjoy their lives. But that survey looked at people's perceptions of others' happiness. What do small-town residents say about themselves?

Surprisingly, another study found little difference between metropolitan and non-metropolitan residents in their perceptions of their own well-being and life satisfaction. The percentage of country folk who were happy with their lives was no greater than the percentage of city folk. Call it the "small-town perception gap"—a difference between the realities of small-town life and urban perceptions of it. One goal of this book is to narrow that gap.

This study went on to suggest that a person's perception of his or her well-being may be more influenced by factors such as financial status, marital status and education. That may be uncomfortable news, if you see the small town as the solution to all of your problems. But what it suggests is that the small-town lifestyle is simply one component of a road to happiness, a road that might be summarized using the words "traditional American values" (especially if it's a conservative politician doing the summarizing). But regardless of your politics, who can argue with this recipe: a happy marriage, sufficient education and financial security?

Deciding to move: Tom Forman

When Tom Forman first came to this country from Czechoslovakia in the 1940s, he settled in southwestern New Hampshire. He met his wife, Monica, in Milford, and soon after their wedding they moved to the Boston area where he pursued a career in engineering.

In 1994, Tom (who had already "retired" more than once) finally decided he wanted to stop working for money. He and Monica were also ready to give up the work associated with their small house on a large lot in a Boston suburb. They started looking at townhouses.

Initially, they looked in nearby towns, but they weren't comfortable with the finances—Tom would have felt obliged to keep working. Their thoughts soon turned to southwestern New Hampshire. "We knew this area," Tom says. "From our early days, when Monica worked in Peterborough, we'd been here often: walking, skiing, enjoying the countryside." They were also encouraged by the area's cultural offerings, such as concerts, lectures and a puppet theater.

Friends had recently moved to nearby Jaffrey, and the Formans asked if there were many condominiums or townhouses in the area. The answer was "plenty," and soon the Formans had found their home in Peterborough.

"The town has changed surprisingly little," Tom says, "from when we were here in the 40s. Milford, which is a few miles up the road, has changed a lot—it's grown." But in Peterborough, the Formans can still see something of the town that was the setting ("Grovers Corner") for Thornton Wilder's 1938 play *Our Town*.

One of the big elements of the decision to move to a small town, Tom says, is evaluating how you'll do without big-city amenities. "How dependent are you on shopping and things like that?" he says to ask. "In an area like this, you can't get the super-duper espresso coffee. You may find that means more to you than you had thought."

Will you be happier living in a small town? That question may seem silly now, as you contemplate unpleasant aspects of your current life-style. Surely, you think, moving to a small town would improve your life. But Pat Jobes, a sociologist at Montana State University, found that for a surprising number of people, it apparently didn't.

The wise preacher

There's a parable about a minister in a small-town church, known for his sage advice, who was consulted by a family considering moving there. "What are the people like here?" they asked.

"What are they like where you live now?"

"Oh, they're petty and small-minded, bigoted, uneducated, lazy, thoughtless, rude...we just can't stand them."

The minister frowned and admitted, "Well, I'm sorry to say you'll probably find the same type of people here." The family said they appreciated the honest response, and they would not be returning.

Shortly thereafter another family came by with the same question: "What are the people like here?"

And the minister responded the same way: "What are they like where you live now?"

"Oh, they're just wonderful. Generous, kind, thoughtful, caring... we just hate the thought of leaving all our friends."

The minister smiled and said, "Well, I'm happy to say you'll probably find the same type of people here."

Jobes studied migration to the Gallatin Valley, one of Montana's hottest destinations. He found that 20 percent of the people who moved there didn't even make it a full year in their new home. Furthermore, surviving that first year was no guarantee they'd "stick." Only half the migrants stayed more than five years. And four out of every five moved away within 10 years.

Statistics can't speak of motives, but one suspects that most of these 80 percent did not find what they were looking for. Picture their disappointment: having uprooted their lives, suffered the financial and emotional hardships of moving and starting anew, only to find that

Deciding to move: Karen Connelly

"I went to college and grad school in towns of about 5,000 people in upstate New York," says Karen Connelly. "There I got my first taste of the community spirit you can get in a small town." It was a contrast with her upbringing, outside Albany, N.Y. "Where I grew up was very much suburbia; I didn't feel that a sense of community."

After graduation, she lived in Madrid, Spain, and Washington, D.C., for a couple of years each. But she quickly decided that urban life was simply not for her. She longed for the access to recreational opportunities and sense of community found in a small town.

"Yellowstone National Park recruits for concessions jobs from all over the U.S.," she says. "It's not at all glamorous or high-paying—I had to save up money in advance—but it provided job security and housing. I was able to use Yellowstone as a base to explore the West.

"I looked for a small town with a large number of activities I like: everything from my book club to recreation, such as hiking and skiing." She settled on Jackson Hole, Wyo. "Jackson is a great combination of culture and athletics. I actually have more options here than I did in D.C.—outdoor activities are so convenient here."

The job market and accessibility were other factors in her decision. "Some of the other places I looked at were college towns," she says, "providing a constant source of cheap labor. And Jackson also has an airport nearby for family visits."

"I waitressed in Jackson when I first arrived," she says. "I was 26 years old and had never waitressed before. But I knew that many businesses in small towns hire based on people they know. They don't do national searches. So I waited on tables while I did interviews."

She landed a job with the Jackson Hole Chamber of Commerce. "I'm fortunate to have found a challenging and exciting job, related to my experience," she says. The job pays enough for her to meet the cost of living. As a resort, Jackson (unlike many small towns) is no cheaper than the city. "A lot of people who've had to leave have said how expensive housing is here. It's probably comparable to D.C."

"I was lucky," she says. "I went to grad school before I moved—that's an option you simply don't have once you're here." She's also firmly aware how much work is involved in setting up a new life...and that its benefits can be a product as much of that work as of the surroundings. "I think perseverance helped me," she says. "I was willing to do what it took to stay here. That develops character."

they weren't happy. They couldn't make enough money. They (or other family members) missed old friends, relatives, culture or landscapes. Or they came to the realization that, as Jobes put it, "Pretty scenery doesn't solve your personal problems."

Picture again the disappointment of these individuals (these four out of every five) and their predicament. Do they go back to where they moved from, admitting their fantasies of small-town life were a mirage? Do they go on to another location, pursuing an unachievable vision of "happiness"? And now ask yourself again, *Would I be happier in a small town? Why?*

20 Questions:
What do you want?

1. Do new situations energize, or frighten you?

2. Do you like your job? How hard would it be to give it up?

3. How much do you like your circle of friends? How important is the time you spend with them?

4. How shy are you? Can you easily find a new circle of friends?

5. How independent are you? Do you like doing things alone?

6. Do you thrive on the bustle and opportunities in the city?

7. Are you an information junkie, knowing news, stock market results or sports scores moments after they're available?

8. Some people feel you're not a success until you've made it in New York City or a similarly cutthroat environment. Do you agree? If not, what's your counter-argument?

9. How will you react when you start seeing animals in the road rather than in the zoo?

10. What is your attitude toward hunters? Commercial fishermen? Farmers? They'd likely be your friends and neighbors.

11. If you have lived in small communities in the past, what did you enjoy about those experiences?

12. What did you dislike about those experiences? How would you counteract those negatives this time?

13. Explain in 20 words or less why you want to move.

14. Explain in a 20-minute conversation why you want to move.

15. List 20 phrases describing your reasons for moving.

16. For each phrase in that list containing the word no, rephrase it as a positive statement.

17. List 20 additional phrases describing concrete, positive attributes of the town you want to live in.

18. How do you expect to be a better (or different) person in the small town?

19. Why will you accomplish that in a small town?

20. Could you accomplish the same objectives without moving?

B. What is small-town life like?

To answer that question, you need to know what your life might be like in a small town. You need this book to confirm (or repudiate) the stereotype of this lifestyle—that vision you find idyllic or frightening (or both). So as a first step, let's articulate this stereotype, paint the full picture. Then we'll go back and study each aspect in detail.

Based on the impressions of most people I've talked to—as well as the impressions I had before making the move myself—I'd wager you envision small towns as having the following characteristics:

- **Safe.** Rates of violent crime—such as murder, rape and muggings—are far lower than in more urban areas.

- **Friendly.** People say hello to you on the street, wave at you through a window or lean across the fence to "visit."

- **Relaxed.** People aren't in as much of a hurry and don't expect you to be either.

- **Gossipy.** Everyone knows everything that everybody else does.

- **Conformist.** Everyone in town does all the same things and, worse, thinks exactly the same way.

- **Boring.** There is absolutely nothing to do. No entertainment, no culture. You'll be crawling the walls within days.

- **Remote.** Specifically, there's nowhere to shop, no way to acquire the "basic necessities" of life.

- **Married.** It will be impossible to find a mate because there are no single people.

- **Religious.** The church is the center of town, geographically, socially, even intellectually.

- **Filled with characters.** One of out every three residents is some crusty old geezer whose great stories almost make up for odd habits and bad hygiene.

- **Agrarian and self-sufficient.** The other residents are all farmers who raise everything they need to live on.

- **Backward.** None of the farmers or geezers graduated from high school. None can conjugate a verb, evaluate a balance sheet or decipher a blueprint.

- **Clean.** There's typically less litter on the streets, less pollution in the air or water.

- **Quiet.** Rarely is your sleep interrupted by sirens.

- **Cheap.** The cost of living is much less than in major urban areas. You can live on practically nothing.

As with any less-than-fully informed impressions, each of these contains both truth and error. In some cases there's more of one than another. But let's tackle each impression in turn.

Popular culture: Groundhog Day

The movie *Groundhog Day* (made in 1993) gets a lot of comic mileage out of Bill Murray's perennially stuck predicament. Murray plays a self-centered Pittsburgh weatherman stuck in Punxsutawney, Penn., to cover the Feb. 2 activities. Due to some odd time warp, every day when he awakes, it's Groundhog Day again. The movie really hits home, however, because that repetition is such a factor in small town life. Nothing changes. Every day is just like the previous day. It's easy to imagine how the repetition of routine could fool an urban visitor into thinking there was indeed a time warp.

The plot of the movie involves Murray's attempt to understand and get out of the time warp. Its laws allow him, but nobody else, to remember what happened in the last go-round. He eventually comes to see this as a blessing rather than a curse; at first he uses the blessing for "selfish" motives such as scoring with women, but eventually he turns to healthier pursuits. He starts taking music lessons. He becomes involved in the town's institutions and meets (and charms) many of its leading citizens. He eventually uses this selflessness to find romantic happiness with his producer, played by Andie Macdowell. These are, as you'll discover, many of the same lessons being preached by this book. When you give of yourself to the community, it will give back to you a sense of belonging and, eventually, happiness.

In a final romantic gesture, the movie's happy couple, saved from the time warp by love, declares that they will move to Punxsutawney. But in an unusual move for a romantic comedy, the movie is also wise enough to know that this might not work. Murray's character is aware that, in the long run, perhaps his character just won't fit in the small town. (For one thing, there's the question of what a TV weatherman and producer would do for work.) Though he's changed somewhat, he still may possess too much cynicism to form bonds with these people, too much drive to be happy in this equivalent of a time warp. His final line (also a recommendation of this book): "We'll rent first."

1. Safe

There's little doubt that small towns are much safer than cities in their freedom from violent crime. As Tom Bruno of Mt. Vernon, Ill., says,

"In these days, I don't think you can say any community is safe. But this is safer. *Everybody knows everybody else.*"

Lisa Rogak, editor of *Sticks*, a newsletter "for people who are serious about moving to the country," writes, "Virtually all of the crime committed in my region involves people who know each other—*real* well." In the city, she notes, you can hope for safety in numbers: By living close to a lot of other people, you can hope the neighbors can rescue you from a burglar or a "loony." In the country, the loonies generally keep to themselves. If you want to live on a back road in the country, she suggests, concerns about the safety of that isolation shouldn't stop you. (Concerns about the loneliness of that isolation, perhaps, should.)

The lack of crime gives you a far greater peace of mind and freedom of activity than you may possess in the city. (Though often, once you've experienced this peace and freedom, you wonder how anyone can live without it.) You can walk around your neighborhood at night. You don't have to lock up the house when you go to bed or when you go out to run an errand. And while running that errand, you don't have to lock your car. My first week living in a small town, the police chief was quoted in the newspaper as saying that as he walked to work one morning, he found that 70 percent of the vehicles on the street had keys in the ignition. He urged citizens to be more responsible—not by locking the car, but by simply taking the key out of the keyhole.

Of course this varies by small town. Growing areas, especially resorts, often have higher crime rates than "backwaters," particularly for burglary and pickpocketing. Some regions may have a tradition of violence; economic stagnation may lead members of other towns to criminal acts. Some rural areas may attract self-styled anti-government radicals stockpiling weapons for a coming revolution. And when crime does occur in any rural area, it can have significant reverberations. You're more likely to be acquainted with both the victim and the perpetrator. Wherever you go in town, people will be talking about it. There's no escape. The tiniest criminal act can be like a pebble dropped in a small pond—you can see its ripples everywhere.

Small towns are strangers to many types of urban crime. Kevin Mastellon's comment about the perceived gang invasion, "They don't know from gangs," bears this out. Acts of vandalism or harassment by groups of youths can cause some small-town Chicken Littles to declare that "gang activity is here." There are exceptions, and the exceptions will probably increase as gang activity, like any fad, moves from the cities to the heartland. But in general, for now, these so-called gangs rarely possess the heavy arms, drug access, lack of regard for human life and general hopelessness and despair of their inner-city counterparts.

Gangs are not the only perpetrators of urban crime. Murders, rapes, muggings, purse-snatchings and burglaries are committed by all sorts of urban "freelancers." Again, these individuals are much less frequently found in small towns, and their crimes are far less likely to occur. Statistics regularly demonstrate this in dispassionate fashion. Sometimes an anecdote can bring it home better: In Vicksburg, Miss., I read a front-page newspaper story analyzing the trends among the city's murders in the previous year. There had been a grand total of three.

While on the subject of safety, we should note that crime is not the only contributor to unsafe conditions. Threats to your health and well-being can also come from traffic accidents, bad working conditions and acts of God. In these categories, the small town does not fare so well. Small town residents drive more...and longer distances. Winding and/or hilly roads, often poorly plowed of snow and ice, also contain more hazards, such as wildlife. So rural people are more likely to get into severe traffic accidents. Furthermore, because there are fewer passers-by and medical care is more remote, victims of traffic accidents in the country are more likely to die from their injuries.

The rate of workplace accidents is also higher in rural areas, because the type of work available (such as farming, mining, logging and small manufacturing) is inherently more dangerous than city jobs (which are largely office jobs). Again, when these injuries occur far from medical care, they are more likely to cause death. (The agricultural sector is notoriously dangerous in this regard.)

Small town people often spend more time outdoors, which many people find to be a healthier lifestyle but not necessarily a safer one. Hiking, hunting and skiing, for example, are filled with potential opportunities to stress or break bones and ligaments. Your children may play in the woods or fields, but at the risk of encountering snakes or rodents that bite. If you worry about such things, moving to a small town may not allay all of your safety fears. In a small town, your child may be less likely to be kidnapped, but more likely to fall down an abandoned mine shaft. Both possibilities, of course, are quite remote. But many people worry obsessively about them nevertheless.

Safety: Kevin Mastellon

"We have an atmosphere where you don't have to lock your car or your house," says Kevin Mastellon of Watertown, N.Y. "You don't need multiple bolts on the doors or alarms on the house. There's no fear of anything really happening."

Kevin should know about crime: He reported on it as an anchor and news director for 15 years before becoming general manager of a Watertown television station. "We'd have an occasional murder," he says, "but they were 'stupid murders'—never a clean hit, always sloppy. In this type of place, burglary is a major crime."

For Kevin, who was born in Brooklyn and raised in Queens, it's a big change. "We do have what people have called 'gang activity,' but, to use an old neighborhood expression, 'they don't know from gangs.' It's a few kids who hang out together. Not switchblade-carrying people getting into fights in alleyways. These are kids who maybe throw their muscle around a bit, then go play basketball."

He is aware that the safety issue revolves around perceptions. "To some extent the cities get a bad rap. I was never attacked in New York City. But around here, you're more worried about being shot by a hunter who thinks you're a deer than being mugged. This brings a tremendous comfort level."

He moved to upstate New York in college, studying computer science at the State University of New York in Potsdam. He got involved in college radio, which led to his career in broadcasting.

"The pace is slower here," he says. "People are less frenetic. We do miss the theater opportunities and professional sports, going to Shea for a Mets game or the Rangers or Knicks at the Garden. We didn't avail ourselves all that often, but it was a nice treat, several times a year."

The Mastellons enjoy the natural beauties of the upstate area, including the Thousand Islands and the Adirondack Mountains. He notes, "Watertown is a nice place to raise a child. Our daughter is musically inclined and the public schools here have an outstanding music program. Though we're Catholic, we sent her to public schools rather than the Catholic school to take advantage of that."

He also cites the friendliness of the community. "You know the mailman, the paperboy, people in stores—you know them by their first names," he says. "People walk with their heads up. They smile and say hi to each other. People talk about whether it's been a hard winter. They don't really 'bitch' about it, they just talk."

Finally, natural disasters pose a serious threat to residents of small towns and big cities alike. As you flee one type of natural disaster—say, a California earthquake—you may be heading for another. The Atlantic and Gulf coasts are hurricane country. Tornadoes hound the southern Midwest. Hail peppers the Plains. Wildfires threaten the West. Devastating floods are a factor throughout the Midwest. You might weigh against these dramatic events the many deaths caused by very cold or very hot weather, not to mention the hassles—not life-threatening but certainly life-diminishing—of bugs or a lack of winter daylight.

In many respects your personal habits (Do you smoke? Do you wear seatbelts? Do you eat fatty foods?) may have a greater effect on your health and safety than so-called acts of God. Personal habits may even outweigh such quantifiable factors as murder rates, the number of physicians in an area or the presence of a hospital. On the other hand, when we speak of safety, we're often looking at the degree to which we feel we have control over our lives. We feel less safe in a crime-infested area or far from a hospital because our lives could be diminished by a crime or an auto accident that isn't our fault. In that sense, the quest for safety—the desire to have and take more responsibility for your life—is an extremely healthy one.

2. Friendly

The stereotype of small towns as friendly places is generally true. "Neighborliness" is often cited by residents as the single most important feature of their town, the reason they love this lifestyle. Even residents of very scenic areas or those with lots of recreational opportunities are more apt to cite a "friendly, small-town atmosphere" as paramount.

Here's a poem about small-town life. Written by Jackie Olson of Washburn, N.D., and published in the May 4, 1995 *Bismarck Tribune,* it struck me as interesting because it's typical of the way small-town residents view their communities:

You know you're in a small town

When you don't use your turn signal because everyone knows where you're going,

When you dial a wrong number and talk 15 minutes anyway,

When you can't walk for exercise because every car that passes you offers you a ride.

As the poem suggests, friendliness is tied to the small size. People offer rides and chat with misdialed phone numbers partly because they're not in a hurry to do something else, but also because they know the other person. In a small town you often look at every car driving by, waving at a large percentage of them, because you recognize not just your friends but the cars they drive. Sometimes the best way for a small-town resident to gain temporary anonymity is to buy a new car.

"People in a small town are easier to get to know," says Ron Mullins, "because you see them everywhere. You see them daily, rather than once a week or once a month." When you've seen a person on consecutive days at the hardware store, grocery store and city council meeting, it becomes quite easy to find common ground with them. (Note, however, that this depends on getting out into the community. If you hole up at home all day long, you won't see people and get to know them.)

Longevity is another factor contributing to friendliness. With little turnover in the small town, you generally know people better, longer. It's not just that you see people daily; you see them every day for your entire life. And you enjoy that: The other residents of your town become like an extended family. Of course you'll be friendly to them. Furthermore, since the small town is filled more with people you know than with strangers, and since you're in the habit of being friendly, you'll be friendly with the strangers, too.

This is one of the biggest differences of small-town life. Small-town residents acknowledge strangers when they pass on the street. They'll look directly at them, instead of down at the ground or off to the side. If their eyes meet (sometimes even if their eyes don't meet), they'll nod or say hello. In Manhattan, of course, the sheer numbers of pedestrians would make this physically impossible; the smaller population of the small town allows these greeting rituals.

Though it may seem minor, these greeting rituals are in fact important to small-town residents. Acknowledging the humanity of a mere stranger on the street seems to elevate both of you, acknowledging in this minor way the ties that bind all of us together. And since you don't have to avoid the eyes of people passing you on the sidewalk, you're able to walk with your head up, rather than buried in the concrete. It can be surprising what a positive difference that makes in your attitude.

Of course any place has its grouches and jerks. And some places have more of them than others. But in a small town, even the grouches and jerks may find themselves nodding at acquaintances. The sense of community that pervades a small town creates friendliness, one of the major benefits of small-town life.

Friendliness: Ron Mullins

"I'll walk around the neighborhood with my family and we'll stop and talk to everyone on the way," says Ron Mullins of Hobbs, N.M. "It takes twice as long as it would just to walk. And that's okay. Because things aren't as rushed here."

Ron, a bank president, was raised in a small town and then lived in the larger cities of Abilene and Albuquerque before being transferred to Hobbs. "In the city, I didn't feel we had neighbors like we did when we were growing up," he says. "In the city people are too busy, not willing to spend time getting to know each other. Here, the community accepts you."

He found Hobbs to be quite open to newcomers. "It is a transient community," he says. "This is oil and gas country here, and we have lots of layoffs. So the town accepts people well. It doesn't take long to get to know people, because they know so many are transient— they'll only be here for one to three years."

Even so, the move can be traumatic, he says, especially for a spouse. "My advice to the spouse is be patient for the first year. There have been people I've hired, and other professionals in town, who didn't last because of pressure from a spouse. My wife experienced similar problems."

Ron's advice to both husband and wife: Get involved. "Don't wait to be asked. Pick something and get involved. The local chamber of commerce is the heartbeat of civic involvement. Start by attending their meetings. It's easy to get involved. They constantly need volunteers. There are an equal number of things to be involved with, but fewer people. So you can see involvement with immediate results.

"And if a program or service doesn't exist, get with civic leaders to see if you can start it. But don't sit back feeling sorry for yourself. Take the initiative. Go out and meet people."

The rewards, he says, can be significant. "In our four years here, we've developed two, three, maybe four times the number of close friends we would have in the city. Because of the size of the community, we've been able to get to know people easily."

3. Relaxed

Small towns have an easier pace than big cities. They're away from the hustle and stress (and stimulation). Some small towns don't seem to change for decades—since nothing ever happens, you never need to play catch-up. People rarely feel rushed in a small town. They can (and do) stop to chat with an acquaintance on the street for 10 minutes.

Sometimes the relaxed pace can be deceiving. Small-town people may have plenty to do, but they value that laid-back facade. They're supposed to get some work done today, but members of the community find it more important to chat with people on the street.

Some small towns thus approach the "mañana" attitude so famous in Mexico. "I'll get to it tomorrow" may not mean the day immediately following today. For various reasons, the electrician, roofer, plumber or snowplower who was supposed to show up on Thursday may not make it until next week.

Small-town culture excuses—even supports—this philosophy because it allows the electrician and roofer to get the same lifestyle benefits out of the town that everyone else does. Community is paramount, and nobody would think of excluding anyone from the opportunity to stop and "visit." (The relaxed atmosphere is a "perk" that makes up for the electrician's comparatively lower wages.)

There are exceptions, of course. If it's an emergency, you can tell the plumber that raw sewage is spewing into your living room and (ideally) get service relatively soon. But often there's only one plumber in town—which means whoever he had scheduled for this morning is going to be postponed until after your emergency. However, with the trust built into the small community, that person will understand the plumber had to attend to your emergency.

When everyone's on the same frequency, the system works quite well. The carpenter will come by to do your indoor project on the first rainy day of next month. The photographer will develop your kids' senior pictures once the tourist rush subsides. Whatever service *you* provide to the community can also be accommodated to other demands on your lifestyle.

On the other hand, outside deadlines can be a problem, especially for businesses accustomed to current society's focus on instant information. Fax machines and overnight delivery are quite foreign to the small-town philosophy. While this is beginning to change, the change may not be fast enough for some "high-powered" people. For example, the small town stretches the meaning of the word "overnight." In my town, only one company offers next-day delivery service, and its deadline is noon. Business people accustomed to working on a project until 10 p.m. before racing it off to the overnight drop-box would find that a difficult transition.

The relaxed atmosphere extends to dress. People don't dress up in a small town. Often you can count on one hand the number of men who wear ties to work. (On the way to a job interview one day, I stopped at the cafe wearing a suit. The owner looked at me and asked, "Who died?") Many people, tired of wearing a "monkey suit" to work every day, will find this a desirable attribute.

But remember that the lack of dress clothes extends to every element of society. People regularly wear blue jeans to parties, cultural events and even church. If you enjoy dressing up or being around people who dress up, you will be frustrated.

Your appreciation for nice clothes may even work against you. When Robyn Kratzer went to a chamber of commerce social soon after moving to Park City, Utah, she consciously "dressed down" in a pantsuit and blouse. "But a friend pulled me aside and said, 'I feel like you won't be offended if I tell you this—we know each other well enough—you are *severely* overdressed.'" Kratzer's collection of great leather shoes has to sit in the closet because they have neither the traction nor the toughness to stand up to winter weather.

And finally, the relaxation holds for traffic as well. Traffic is one of the most frequently condemned components of metropolitan living—by both urban and rural folk alike. Small-town people are constantly amazed at the traffic of southern California or northern New Jersey, because there is absolutely nothing comparable in a small town.

Small-town residents may drive slowly on a country road to enjoy the scenery or because the tractor doesn't go any faster, but major thoroughfares aren't congested with stop-and-go traffic. (There are exceptions during tourist season in some recreational meccas.) In a small town, the stop-and-go traffic is of a different nature: You stop for pedestrians on the crosswalk. Meanwhile, pedestrians return the favor: They generally cross at the corner, waiting for a light if there is one, instead of maneuvering one lane at a time in the middle of the block.

4. Gossipy

We've been discussing some of the positive aspects of small-town living: safety, friendliness, relaxation. Let's switch now and examine some of the characteristics that are not so widely admired. For example, small towns are seen as terribly gossipy.

When Tom Bruno moved to Mt. Vernon, Ill., to manage the Ramada Inn, he says, "I was shocked at the number of people who knew me. They knew my name and I had no idea who they were." A newcomer can be a rare event in the small town, worthy of talking about. Depending on the size and popularity of the town you move to, you may be one of a few dozen or just three or four people moving into town all year.

You may be a celebrity without having done anything worthwhile to warrant it. If you're not comfortable with that—if it makes your skin crawl to think that people might be talking about you—you may have trouble in the small town.

Gossip is a byproduct of the close-knit community. Its effects can be destructive, no doubt. But it's a quality you can't simply eradicate. Gossip is the flipside of safety and security. We love a small town because it's the kind of place where the neighbors notice that elderly Mrs. Witherspoon hasn't opened her curtains like she usually does, so they go check to see if she's ill. And we hate a small town when those same neighbors notice that Jeannie's boyfriend spent the night. But it's the same behavior. The two go hand-in-hand. People don't have very many neighbors; they know their neighbors and they pay attention to their neighbors' lives.

Keep in mind that there's a difference between knowledge and tolerance. Some communities will be more tolerant than others of Jeannie's sleeping arrangements. In Chapter 2, we'll examine ways you can investigate this level of tolerance.

"It's like living in a fishbowl," says Diane Heady-Reuss of Stockbridge, Mass. "But there are benefits, too, that far outweigh the minuses. Everyone knows your business, but once you get past a certain point, that becomes basically irrelevant."

In short, your secrets will probably become known. On the other hand, there may be worse things than having your neighbors familiar with your life.

Gossip: Tom Bruno

Tom Bruno has some advice for someone considering moving to a small town: "Be prepared: People will know who you are."

When he first moved to Mt. Vernon, Ill., he says, he was accosted by strangers. "At the grocery store or the post office, people I didn't know would ask me how things were going at the hotel. I realized I'd better not do anything wrong or the whole town would know it. But of course I had to get to know 17,000 people, and they only had to get to know one."

Tom grew up in St. Louis and lived in Pensacola, Fla., and Tyler, Texas, before moving to Mt. Vernon to manage the Ramada Inn. "It's more stable here," he says of his new home. "We were also glad to be closer to St. Louis. And in the smaller community, it's easier to keep tabs on our four young children."

But he also advises that the move can take a lot of energy. "It *is* an adjustment," he says. "Not a bad adjustment, but an adjustment.

"For example, until recently we had one little mall with a Wal-Mart, not a lot of variety. We still have just one grocery store—it's a nice store, but you just don't have the choices you might in a larger city."

Day-to-day activities also require an adjustment, he says. "In St. Louis, we might go to a ballgame, the zoo or other big-city activities. Here I go jogging or play softball—there's not as much to do. It takes about 15 minutes to walk through the mall."

His wife, he notes, also had a big adjustment. She was busy with the children and at first had trouble making friends. But now she knows several other mothers and has gotten involved in school activities. The close-knit, small community works as well for her as it does for him. "In fact," he says, "at this point, she and the kids are the main reason I'd like to stay."

5. Conformist

Perhaps the chief negative stereotype of small town life is its conformity. A small town doesn't allow freedom of expression, freedom of lifestyle. It doesn't tolerate weirdness or artistic talent. If you don't conform to its rigid standards of success and proper behavior, you'll be shunned or driven out of town.

Some great artists have been frustrated in small towns. Novelist Sinclair Lewis's, most acclaimed novels (including *Main Street* and *Babbitt*) exposed the conformity of the small Minnesota town where he had been raised. Lewis escaped that town as soon as he could and made his home in artistic communities in New York City and Europe.

Even artists who celebrate small town life don't always live there. Wallace Stegner, acclaimed as the greatest voice of the rural West, spent most of his career in the more urban setting of Stanford University. Likewise, Norman Maclean lived in Chicago for most of his working life before retiring to his native Montana to write *A River Runs Through It*. Tony Hillerman's acclaimed mysteries are set in rural Navajo country, but the author lives in Albuquerque. The list goes on.

Though many artists *do* live in small towns, such as William Faulkner or the visual artists who put Taos, N.M., on the map, the commonly held belief that small towns don't tolerate artists does have some truth to it. Struggling artists, even bad artists, are likely to find more appreciation *for their art* in a more cosmopolitan setting. However, a small town's support for the artist's lifestyle or subject material could outweigh the conformity factor. (For example, consider a landscape painter, a nature writer or a "small-town person" who also happens to earn a living making pottery.)

Again, conformity is the flip side of something we value—in this case, the sense of community. We value the small town because of its sense that people are committed to the group, the community. But this means that if someone believes your personal goals are in conflict with the group's, they'll favor the group's goals over yours. The inclusiveness of a well-functioning community rarely includes notions of personal status-seeking. You achieve status through the group, through your value to the group or support of the group. For example, you may be more revered in town for helping put on the Fourth of July parade than for winning a major professional award.

Thus, conflict will arise when (or if) the group's goals are wildly different from your own. The goals of most small towns are to perpetuate the community, to raise children in a safe environment and to live quiet, satisfying lives among like-minded people. There are exceptions, of course: Some communities will have other goals. The need to perpetuate the community might cause some places to conform to environmentalism and others to free-market capitalism.

The 20th century has rightly seen the advent of equality (or at least tolerance) for a wide variety of minority groups: women, Blacks, other ethnic or racial minorities, gays, lesbians and people with a variety of "alternative lifestyles." These changes necessarily came from urban areas, which focus on opportunity and lack small-town conformity. Certainly the changes of tomorrow will come from cities as well. Some small towns (in general, those that have been exposed to the outside world) have caught up to the rest of society in this regard. Others (those that have perpetuated white male dominance) possess the worst features of a time warp.

The conformity of the small town does allow the group to transmit *values* to its young. Again, this is a double-edged sword. We like "values" when it means the community will help us raise our children to respect hard work. But we decry "conformity" when nobody in town will hire one of our teenage sons because he has a reputation of not working hard. You need to decide which you find more important: the values of community life or the opportunities available in a larger city.

In some small towns, there's a perception that the rest of the community doesn't want you to succeed. Everyone else gangs up to tear down someone who has "gotten too big for his britches," even when that means only modest financial success. I've never encountered this phenomenon, though I've heard enough about it to accept that it must be true in some places.

Certainly it's true of the ostentatious display of wealth. Many small towns look down on material objects that seem to serve more as trophies than for their original intended use. A car or a house should be practical—for driving or living in—rather than display wealth or status. Often your car or truck will be admired for the size and number of things it can carry than for its high price, engineering or design. The same can apply to furniture, clothing and accessories.

But the uneasiness with wealth may have a deeper cause as well. As an independent economic unit, the small town has always provided goods and services to itself. Thus, the car dealer, banker and grocery store owner must all belong to Rotary (or a similar civic club) for business reasons. These are their potential customers. In larger cities, economic criteria are paramount, as a car buyer looks for the best deal. But in the small town, each businessperson's livelihood has traditionally depended on the web of community.

Popular culture: A Prairie Home Companion

Garrison Keillor starts off the monologue on his weekly public radio show with the line, "It's been a quiet week in Lake Wobegon." He uses the refrain for its subtle humor—it's something small-town people all around the country say. Even though it's been a quiet week, Keillor goes on to talk for 15 minutes about what *has* happened in Lake Wobegon. In these stories, what happened this week frequently blends in with what happened months, years or generations ago. The events of city life can be broken into specific chunks (this week we had four fires, two murders and one political scandal) that seem to arise suddenly in media attention and then disappear. In small towns, events, causes and effects all seem to blend together, creating processes (and stories) that are difficult to pinpoint in time.

The show is popular, especially in the Midwest, because Lake Wobegon is so accurate. There's the focus on family and its various interrelationships, yet also a sense that the whole community is part of an extended family. Keillor is updating us, the distant aunts and uncles, on the family's latest escapades. Note also the regular gathering of upstanding citizens at the "Chatterbox Cafe" and the less-upstanding citizens at the tavern. And there's the heavy social influence of the church.

Lake Wobegon is full of characters—or at least its stories are. Residents are always doing ever-so-slightly daffy things that make them both endearing and interesting. Though there is a great deal of conformity and some public pressure to conform, the community's long-term, trusted residents often do something strange or even stupid. They are tolerated and forgiven by their neighbors (who, after all, might be the ones doing something stupid next week) and particularly by Keillor, the storyteller.

Keillor's storytelling ability has a great deal to do with our affection for Lake Wobegon. The events that strike us as so funny or touching in his monologues might not strike the participants as funny or touching (had they really happened). The participants would see their lives as quite humdrum. A visitor in Lake Wobegon, or someone thinking about moving there, might pass through or even spend several weeks there without seeing anything "noteworthy." They would, in fact, regularly report that it has been a very quiet week indeed.

Note, however, the implications of this traditional interdependence. If the car dealer is getting rich, he must be doing so off of you and me. At our expense. We go to him because he's the only car dealer in town and we value the sense of community, but he takes advantage of that community spirit to enhance his personal status. He has violated the "rules" of community, and we are right to resent him.

Economic patterns are changing. You can now acquire your wealth off of somebody outside of your small-town community. But the social mores may take a while to catch up and, in the interim, others may continue to be uneasy about that wealth and may want to "tear you down" because you somehow "don't deserve it."

Levels of conformity can differ in different communities. Generally, across society, levels of conformity are getting looser as tolerance for alternatives increases.

Many people, however, seem to prefer high levels of conformity. They move to suburbs where your ZIP code can predict the type of toothpaste you use. Or they move to planned residential communities, many of which have rules about children, pets, trucks, trailers, landscaping or the color you can paint your house. In such communities, of course, the conformity is outwardly stated, written in covenants and restrictions, rather than being a tacit agreement among old-timers. Nevertheless, the demand for conformity is great. And nonconformists may find themselves more at home in a funky small town than a subdivision of identical buildings filled with identical people. In moving to a small town, you want to judge not the existence of conformity (because it's everywhere) but its tenets. What do the people conform to? If the community's goals and ideals are socially, politically or morally different from yours, then yes, you will have conflicts and problems in that community. (Of course, to say you'll have conflicts is not to say you'll be unhappy.) If there's support or tolerance for your goals and ideals, you may not find conformity to be any more of an issue than it was in your previous residence.

An important difference: Unlike most other communities, small towns are geographically isolated. It's difficult to get away from the conformity. In a metropolitan area, you may be a member of conformist groups at your work place, in your neighborhood and among your friends. But they're three different groups. If you live in a ski town, skiers are your co-workers, neighbors and friends, all three. Come the beginning of ski season, you will find it impossible to avoid conversations about skiing. If you don't like to ski, you may indeed find the conformity stifling. The same obviously applies for the central facet of any small town: agriculture, fishing, timber, religion or ethnic heritage. Perhaps what we fear most about small-town conformity is the difficulty of switching brands.

6. Boring

How will you ever find anything to do in a small town? Isn't it oppressively dreary?

Well, maybe. Whether or not you find anything to do in a small town depends a great deal on what you like to do.

Tom Bruno found it a bit dull, not being able to go to a major mall or a ballgame. On the other hand, Karen Connelly found it exciting being closer to recreational opportunities, such as hiking and skiing. The difference is accounted for by their different interests.

First of all, let's dispense with the obvious. There's no doubt a small town has nowhere near the **culture** of the city. Moving to a small town, you seriously diminish your opportunities to take advantage of:

• Major league sports.

• Top-notch theater.

• Symphonies.

• Top-notch rock, folk, jazz or blues shows.

• Big-name lecture series.

• Outstanding museums.

• Varieties of restaurants, particularly ethnic restaurants.

• Opportunities for higher education.

Which is not to say you give up everything. In a university town, particularly, you may find theatrical and intellectual offerings. For Mary Beasley, living in the university town of Oxford, Miss., is a cultural cornucopia. Outstanding art museums exist in towns with populations under 15,000, such as Taos, N.M.; Cody, Wyo.; and Williamstown,

Mass, but you may find the offerings limited compared to most metropolitan areas, which offer *multiple* universities and museums.

Small towns are often bereft of even decent radio. Do you listen to an all-news station? All sports? Classical? Folk? Jazz? Alternative rock? If you're lucky, you'll move to a small town with all six of those combined on one public radio station. If you're lucky. Otherwise, your choices will be classic rock, soft rock or country. And you'll probably tire of them soon.

Let's say that you move to a small town renowned for its culture. It may have one, maybe two good museums. It may catch a touring theater company four times a year or present numerous offerings during a short festival. It may have a college with an acclaimed music department putting on concerts three or four times a semester. But total up the number of events you could attend over the course of a year, 104 Saturdays and Sundays. Is it enough? How does it compare to the number of events you take in now? Taking full advantage of the town's cultural resources, would you still find yourself complaining, "There's nothing to do"?

If cultural activities are important to you, you may want to plan yearly, quarterly or monthly pilgrimages to a big city. You may want that city nearby, so you don't spend lots of money and time traveling there. (But choose your big city as carefully as you do your small town. Don't assume that just because a city has 200,000 residents it'll have the cultural opportunities of a Boston or San Francisco.) In a long weekend, you might be able to get in enough to save you until the next trip.

On the other hand, if regular *access* to such cultural activities is important to you, you may want to give up on moving to a small town. Many people gain comfort knowing that on any given day they could pop down to a museum—even if they only act on such wishes once or twice a year. Such spur-of-the-moment trips are impossible from the small town. (The opposite is also true: Many small-town residents gain comfort in knowing that on any given day they could go for a swim in the lake—though only occasionally acting on such impulses. The city folk get by with an occasional planned vacation in the country; the country folk get by with an occasional planned visit to the city.)

Similarly, if the *level* of cultural activities is important to you, you may find a small town frustrating. What do you like about a baseball game? Watching a superstar such as Ken Griffey, Jr., hit a home run?

Entertainment: Mary Beasley

"Surely nobody should be bored here," says Mary Beasley of Oxford, Miss. "There's so much going on in one evening that often you can't do it all."

Mary had lived outside of Buffalo, N.Y., before problems in the steel industry forced her husband into early retirement. They spent a winter with their son in Gulfport, Miss., where Mary started caring for two young children, a job she enjoyed very much. They followed her employer to Jackson and then Oxford.

"After we'd been here six months," Mary says, "we loved Oxford so much we wanted to stay."

What clicked about Oxford? "The biggest surprise was the variety of cultural activity here. Its being a college town is a big hit with me. The university arts and music departments have free events—which is wonderful for retirees—almost every week. There are museums, parks and sports. Oxford is also working on getting more bike and walking paths."

She also finds Oxford to be very convenient. "Everything is on the square: city, county and federal buildings, banks, the post office, churches... It's all accessible from one parking place."

Another important factor is that Oxford has some similarity to the lifestyle and landscapes she experienced in upstate New York. "Our typical activities haven't changed much," she says. "We bowled in Buffalo; we bowl here. We enjoyed Lake Erie in Buffalo; we have lakes here. We enjoy swimming; we do a lot with kids.

"A lot of people retire to Florida, but we're not thrilled with Florida. I don't like flat land or sand. Here in Oxford we have four seasons, hardwood trees and rolling hills that remind us of the Buffalo area."

She obviously leads an active retirement. "They have events at the high school, the county hall, the chapel, the museum. There's something for everybody. A lot of brown-bag luncheon events, things at the university or the hospital. Then there's fishing and hunting."

The Beasleys have been in Oxford almost 10 years now, showing few signs of slowing down. She looks back on the move as a completely positive experience. "We had no hardships moving here. Maybe it's because we were flexible enough. But I haven't heard of others having problems either. Many say Oxford feels like coming home."

Or relaxing in the sun with a bag of popcorn? If the latter, then you may enjoy minor league baseball, which is often played in or near small towns. Likewise, if you go to a symphony to see Yo Yo Ma or Seiji Ozawa rather than simply experiencing live classical music, you may be disappointed in the symphonies of small cities or universities.

To determine whether you'll find enough entertainment in the small town, you need to ask yourself how you define entertainment. Though small towns lack the cultural opportunities of urban areas, you may not avail yourself even now of such opportunities. As Kenneth Jackson points out in *Crabgrass Frontier*, a history of suburbia, most Americans don't. They close themselves off in suburban neighborhoods. Meanwhile, the downtown concert halls, opera houses, ballet companies and museums sometimes find themselves squeezed for cash.

Many Americans today find greater enjoyment in playing golf, fixing up their houses or watching television. Even those who claim to enjoy rock concerts, athletic events or breakdancing exhibitions demonstrate their real preferences by spending more of their free time relaxing by the pool or on the patio.

If this describes you, there's good news. Golf courses exist nationwide, though some may not be as challenging, scenic or interesting as you'd like. A small-town house gives you plenty of opportunities to work on fix-it projects or gardening or to build and/or enjoy a patio or pool. Television is also widespread. Though you may have to spring for a satellite dish, improved technology is continually decreasing this cost. (In fact, some people believe that television is eroding the traditional small-town spirit of participation and communal activity, but more on this later.)

So rather than cultural events, perhaps you (like most Americans) are more apt to consume packaged entertainment. You watch television, rent videos, play video games or fiddle with your computer. You're part of the 90s trend of "cocooning"—staying home with your family. If so, you may get along quite well in the small town. The selection of video rentals may not be as good as where you are now, but philosophically you'll fit in quite well. Small-town families have been "cocooning" for years, long before anyone invented a term for it.

One of the big complaints of many people who move to small towns is the lack of "good" **restaurants**. "Good" needs quotation marks because peoples' definitions of restaurant quality can vary. Around the country, you may find holes-in-the-wall with great (and cheap) but simple food. Diners, cafes, barbecue shacks or fish houses might have fresh food cooked in a regional style. If such places are your idea of a good restaurant, you'll probably do well in the small town. In fact, as a newcomer you may even appreciate a "homestyle" restaurant more than the natives, to whom home style is old hat. Of course, the frequency and quality of such places can vary, as Robyn Kratzer found out in Utah.

If you're into a full "dining experience," small-town restaurants may disappoint you. The decor and service are usually not up to the levels of metropolitan restaurants. Many people appreciate dining out not so much for the food but for the rejuvenating experience of having someone wait on you. Food appears (and dirty plates disappear) at the proper times, leaving you free to converse with your spouse or friends. Such experiences are more difficult to find in the small town.

Part of the problem is a lack of demand: With fewer (and poorer) people in a small town, many upscale restaurants don't attract enough customers to stay in business. Since small towns are laid-back places that focus on communal experience, the notion of "good service" doesn't necessarily fit in. Waitresses in small-town restaurants are more likely to banter with you or ask about your kids than to demurely set down your plate, refill your water and wait for your gratuity.

Furthermore, your choice may be limited. There may be just one ethnic restaurant. And "ethnic" may mean "bad Mexican food." Country people tend to have conservative tastes. They may like fried or fatty foods and may be slow to adopt new trends. In some rural areas, what they call a bagel more closely resembles a piece of Wonder Bread shaped like a donut. You might be able to get a great steak in town, but if you tire of steak—or if you want a vegetarian meal—you may be out of luck.

While a "dining experience" plays a diminished role in small town life, **bar and tavern** experiences play a larger role. Often, the purpose of these institutions is not just "decadence" but to serve as a larger gathering-place and social outlet. In very small towns, the bar, restaurant, gas station and convenience store may all be located in the same building. So when you stop in for gas or milk, you may stay for a cup of coffee...or a beer. In some towns, bars are multigenerational. Children are welcome. The establishment serves nonalcoholic beverages for kids and other nondrinkers.

Entertainment: Robyn Kratzer

"Here, you don't go to movies or galleries or 'freebie' concerts," says Robyn Kratzer, who moved from Houston to Park City, Utah, in 1994. "Here your social time is outdoor sports. There's no ballet—it's golf, tennis, skiing, hiking or mountain biking. Social dynamics revolve around outdoor activities."

Robyn and her husband had considered themselves outdoor people who enjoyed hiking and camping. But the magnitude of the change caught them by surprise.

"I had no casual clothes," she says. "I had to buy a whole new wardrobe." The fashionable clothes she wore in Houston were now useless. "I couldn't wear leather shoes because they'd get destroyed by the winter weather. Plus I'd fall on the ice—no traction." But her clothing budget didn't decrease at all. "I spent $500 to $600 on winter coats and boots alone. Then I had to buy outdoor gear for skiing and other sports. And then mountain bikes."

Another social difference was restaurants. "You know," she says, "every region of the country has its special food—except this region. In Houston, we had Cajun, Mexican and seafood right there, plus big Middle Eastern and Asian communities with great restaurants. We ate out four or five nights a week.

"Here, we're in the country, so we have to drive half an hour to eat out. And our favorite kind of food, Tex-Mex, just isn't available— believe me, we've tried every Mexican restaurant within 40 miles. We also found the cost of eating out is much higher than Houston." In a resort area she found the cost of most everything to be higher.

Opportunities for shopping were also diminished. In Houston, Robyn had been used to most major department store chains and designer outlets. "Last July, I needed a new dress for a trip. I went to Dillard's because I was familiar with the store. I found a dress I liked, but they didn't have it in my size. I asked if they could call around to the other branches to find my size, but the person who did that was gone for the day. I couldn't wait—I was leaving the next day. So I said, 'Okay, where's the nearest store? I'll drive there.' The girl looked at me dead serious and said, 'Las Vegas.'"

In such sparsely populated areas (this is probably more true in the West than the East or South), bars are simply social outlets. They function like European coffee houses—places to gather and talk. Many country jobs are solitary and many don't use a strict 9-to-5 (or more likely 8-to-4) schedule. Thus, a farmer or salesman may stop in at a bar during the day just to relax and see a friendly face, much like office workers might wander down to the water cooler. So don't be embarrassed to do the same: Stop in on an empty bar at midday. It probably won't be depressing like urban bars. And it won't reveal a character deficiency, unless you start spending all afternoon there every day.

Popular culture: Cheers

The television show *Cheers* was set in a Boston bar where camaraderie rather than alcohol seemed to be the major product dispensed. You could never really tell what time of day it was: midday, after work or later in the evening. The regulars (and some strangers) seemed to inhabit the place much as they would their homes.

In this sense, the *Cheers* bar always struck me as a small-town setting. Living for several years in the Boston area, I never really found a bar with that atmosphere. But I often encounter such bars in small towns.

Of course small-town bars, like all real-life bars, have their share of ugly and/or sad drunks. Indeed, alcoholism is major problem in many rural areas. Such unpleasant characters were, on the other hand, largely excluded from the show.

Like most situation comedies, the show portrayed a community grappling with a variety of crises. Like most situation comedies— whether the community portrayed is a family, workplace or recreational setting—the show and its stories were in many ways idealized and artificial.

Nevertheless, we always look for those idealized elements in real life. In this case, we seek a place that has that level of community among apparent strangers (the characters didn't share family, occupational or other interests). To my mind, the small town—and the small-town bar—come as close as anything to capturing that sense of community.

For many small-town residents, "entertainment" is **participatory**. Music lovers, rather than attending concerts, might sing in a church choir. Sports lovers, rather than attending professional games, might play in a softball league or a weekly volleyball game. Theater buffs might act in a local production. Intellectuals might take or teach an adult education class or participate in a reading circle.

Another form of small-town participatory entertainment is volunteer activities. As Ron Mullins notes, "There are an equal number of things to be involved with, but fewer people." Thus many people who move to a small town get appointed to (or better yet, volunteer for) boards and committees. After a few weeknights of board meetings or helping to clean up and repaint the Civic Center, you may be ready for a quiet night at home, not caring how many cultural activities are available.

Getting involved can also change your perspective on traditional entertainment. "It used to be there was nothing to do in town except go to the bar," said a friend of mine who'd been swept up in a cause. "But now it's great: You go to a meeting and *then* go to the bar." The meetings incited emotions and debates; these spilled over to make discussions and arguments in the bar a great form of participatory entertainment.

Even if you're not participating, your friends and neighbors most likely are. This can add meaning and excitement to an otherwise drab-sounding event. For example, high school sports are great entertainment in the small town because you often know the participants or their families. In this case, of course, the quality of the sport is not as important as who's playing.

You may be impressed with how much more loyalty a local team inspires when you personally know the participants rather than simply reading about their salaries in the newspaper. These reasons of community loyalty are, no doubt, what make Indiana high school basketball and Texas high school football such huge institutions.

The pot-luck dinner is the small town participatory version of eating out at different restaurants. Rather than sampling the cuisine of different chefs, you sample those of your friends and neighbors. The laid-back atmosphere of the small town means that each attendee usually has time to prepare something (unlike the city, where so many people work into the early evening). Small-town informality means that hosting a pot-luck doesn't require a great deal of preparation.

The host might clean house beforehand and wash up afterwards, but needs to prepare only one dish, just like everyone else.

Pot luck

The term "pot luck" may bring images of chicken pot pie and five varieties of Jell-O. That tradition is certainly strong, particularly for church pot lucks, and it can be a fascinating cultural experience.

But in small towns, pot lucks are also fashionable among young people with sophisticated tastes. Certain individuals will develop reputations for bringing particularly tasty salads, breads or vegetarian dishes. Others develop reputations for bringing small or unimaginative dishes but make up for it by eating prodigiously. Some bachelors with no cooking skills can subsist on a diet of potato chips, as long as they're also invited to a lot of pot lucks. Sampling all the food at a big pot luck becomes a dining experience worthy of fancy restaurants.

In my town we often do theme pot lucks such as Mexican or barbecue. We cook some pretty unusual foods. Inspired by an event in Bobbie Ann Mason's novel *In Country*, I once hosted a "white party" where everyone had to wear white and bring white food.

When larger areas adopt pot-luck traditions, they sometimes add a dose of formality. The host keeps track of who's bringing what: two salads, two breads, two desserts and so on. Sometimes a host even assigns dishes based on letters of the alphabet. ("Everyone whose last name begins with A through E, bring a main dish.") But in small towns the informal, haphazard approach is favored—even savored. One of our more famous local events of recent times was the pot luck where 80 percent of the guests brought chips and salsa.

Whatever the theme, whatever the quality, the pot luck embodies the simplicity of small town entertainment: gathering with friends in a home.

You'll want to go to local theater productions, variety shows or art openings—not necessarily because of quality, but community. Oddly, when my local theater started bringing in shows from the nearby city, my interest in attending waned. I wanted to see my friends up there on stage, not some marginally more-talented strangers from the city.

For many people, such as Karen Connelly, access to **outdoor activities** is the reason to live in a small town. As a small-town resident, many outdoor activities are not only more accessible but also seem more in tune with your new lifestyle. These may include any of the following:

- Hiking.
- Mountain biking.
- Road biking.
- Walking.
- Downhill skiing.
- Cross-country skiing.
- Fishing.
- Hunting.
- Swimming.
- Motorboating.
- Water-skiing.
- Sailing.
- Canoeing.
- Kayaking.
- Camping.
- Gardening.
- Recreational driving.
- Hang-gliding.
- Piloting your own plane.
- Bird-watching.
- Observing or photographing wildlife.

Many people move to a small town to take advantage of resources for such passions. Unfortunately, sometimes they then forget or minimize it. They spend so much time trying to earn enough money to afford their beachfront house, for example, that they never get out to the beach. Commitment to such passions can turn out to be harder than you might think.

On the other hand, you may not have passions for such activities. Your preferences may be for urban activities such as museums, sidewalk cafes, high fashion or people-watching. If so, watch out. Moving to a small town will remove you from regular access to these activities.

Residents of resort areas typically take advantage of the recreation offered but not the subsequent party. For example, residents of a ski town may ski all day but skip the *apres-ski*. Or they may not even ski all day, preferring to take advantage of the better conditions and thinner crowds of the early morning hours. Likewise, oceanfront residents may walk on the beach at sunrise or sunset, not joining the big lunch party or afternoon volleyball game. Some resort residents hardly ever take advantage of recreational opportunities but instead gain strength just from knowing they're nearby. They're similar to urban residents who want to be close to museums and galleries even if they only go once a year.

One final note about resort towns: If you're considering moving to one because you love its party atmosphere, keep in mind that once you are a resident, a bar filled with tourists may not hold the same excitement.

7. Remote

As we've seen, small-town people often think of entertainment in different ways than do their big-city cousins. The same can be said for shopping. From a small town, you don't have access to the same variety and quality of shops you do in the big city. And as a result of that (or perhaps it's a cause...), shopping is not as important for small-town people.

If you enjoy the act of shopping as a form of entertainment, you will probably be frustrated by the small town's lack of resources. "In the Midwest there are malls all over the place," says Diane Heady-Reuss, who moved from near Chicago to Stockbridge, Mass. "Here, there's none of it." If the small town has a shopping mall, it may contain only a Kmart and a grocery store. As Robyn Kratzer found, there can be a huge difference between deciding to buy a new set of clothes and actually finding something you like that fits.

Even if you're not a "mall rat," you may still be in for diminished opportunities in the small town. How often do you go to a music store to buy tapes or CDs of your favorite (perhaps obscure) artists? How often do you go to a gigantic bookstore to buy outstanding books (such as the one you're reading right now)? How often do you stroll down shopping-and-architecture enclaves, such as Boston's Newbury Street or Faneuil Hall, or shopping-and-weirdness enclaves, such as LA's Venice Beach? Even people who rarely buy anything often enjoy the atmosphere created by neighborhoods or developments that are nevertheless chiefly geared toward shopping.

In addition to the act of shopping, however, there are the results of shopping. Again, the small town offers limited choices. You don't get fancy coffees, unusual imported vegetables or new gadgets and appliances (be it coffee makers or bread machines). You also don't get the latest fads in clothing, accessories or toys. Fads—everything from frozen yogurt to in-line skates—start in the cities. Eventually they make it to small towns, but only after they've become fully accepted, or even passé, everywhere else.

Services, as well as "things," can be difficult to find in a small town. As Jerry Germer points out in *Country Careers*, you may have trouble finding a piano tuner, an orthodontist or a repair shop for your small, specialized appliance.

Service practitioners or professionals in small towns are typically generalists rather than specialists. There may be no lawyer, for example, specializing in workers' compensation cases. The town may have one lawyer who's happy to take the case, mixed in with her business in wills, real-estate work and drunk-driving cases. (She may well be an excellent attorney. In fact, despite her lack of experience in the subject matter of the case, she may be a better choice for the case than an out-of-town expert because she knows the *context*—the local people and institutions involved.) Likewise, the only doctors in town may be general practitioners.

Of course, for most of your needs a generalist may well be good enough. You may need a lawyer only for wills and real-estate trans-actions and a doctor for physical exams or other simple ailments. (Indeed, finding a "family practice" doctor in a specialist-laden metropolitan area can sometimes be a difficult chore.)

Furthermore, the shopping and services available are likely to be convenient. Mary Beasley found this to be true in Oxford, Miss: "Every-thing is right here on the square," she says. "The county building, city hall, the federal building, banks, the post office, utilities, even churches—I can get to them all from one parking space."

Of course, some products are actually *more* easily available in the country than the city, such as fresh eggs, fresh local produce and other local products, such as maple syrup or seafood. For example, while the small-town grocery may not carry your favorite gourmet ice cream, it may offer fresh local strawberries.

In general, new products simply aren't important to small-town natives. The clothing store doesn't follow fashion trends (or it lags far behind them)—neither do people at local parties. There's no place to get fancy shoes—nobody ever wears them. You can buy things secondhand

and admit it! In a dying small town, one of the last places to close is often the secondhand furniture store. (Meanwhile, in booming small towns, such establishments reposition their merchandise as "antiques.")

Thus, for many small-town residents, the lack of shopping isn't a problem. They may not even be aware that some people see it as a problem. If a career or a spouse moved them to the big city, they still might not avail themselves of shopping opportunities. If you fit this description, or want to, you may do well in the small town.

8. Married

Are you shopping for a mate? Choice may be limited in this regard, too. With the exception of some resorts, small towns have few single people. The single people who do exist tend to be very young or very old.

Small-town residents—especially those who grew up there—are apt to marry young. These are individuals who know what they want: These people want to stay in this town and marry someone else who does, too. Their world is quite small: They may well expect not to meet any additional marriageable members of the opposite sex after they get out of high school. Their idea of traditional values is tied to having babies rather than having adventures. They see no need to delay those dreams.

Meanwhile, many single people who move to a small town from other places often do so to escape or recover from a bad relationship. Maybe they're single parents coming "home" where relatives can help take care of their children. Maybe a divorce or breakup has so scarred them that they need the familiar landscapes and characters of the place where they grew up. Or maybe they're so discouraged about relationships that they have come to a place where they hope not to be bothered. Whatever the reason, many of the (relatively few) people who appear to be single may not be in the market.

This is not to say that you're necessarily doomed to a monastic existence. Well-adjusted, healthy single people do live in small towns and more are moving in as the migration trend grows. Furthermore, if you like living in a small town and you want a mate who shares that interest, you may well be better off looking for him or her in the small town.

Consider how you meet members of the opposite sex. In the small town, you typically get to know them before dating—and after breaking up. If you typically get into relationships with people you've known a while and stay civil with them after it's "over," you may do well in the small town. If you hate the thought of running into an "ex" on the sidewalk or at a party, it'll be harder—not impossible, but harder. In the small town, you're also less likely to go on blind dates or to meet total strangers because you already know everyone in town. Again, study your habits and preferences to see if you'll be a good match for the small town.

But even if you match well, by no means is it easy. In the small town, there are simply fewer single people to choose from. There may simply be no tall, dark-haired 28-year-old college graduates—or no 28-year-olds of *any* height, education or hair color. And of course once you do start dating, everyone knows it. At this point, you may find the gossip of the close-knit community distinctly uncomfortable.

Problems with relationships are probably the second biggest reason people move away from a small town (the biggest being lack of economic opportunities):

• Some leave for lack of a relationship: They decide that in order to meet someone with their interests, they need a bigger, more cultured area.

• Others leave for the needs of a relationship. A spouse's or partner's career may call them elsewhere.

• Other times, a spouse or partner is unhappy socially.

This last reason is particularly true for young married couples starting a family. While she was working, the wife may not have minded the small town. Now that she's home with the baby so much, she realizes how little support she has from long-term friends, contemporaries or family. She may demand to move closer to relatives or to a suburb filled with young families.

9. Religious

Organized religion generally plays a larger role in the lives of small-town residents than it does for those in metropolitan areas. The traditional, community-based lifestyle of the small town typically involves going to church each Sunday. According to a 1995 University of North Dakota poll, 70 percent of North Dakotans pray at least every day (nearly a quarter of them pray more than once a day). And North Dakota is far from the "Bible Belt"—the area of the rural South characterized by particularly strong religious convictions.

So your neighbors will probably be religious. The religion may vary: Lutheran, Catholic or Mormon, depending on the region of the country. And particularly in more tolerant, more heterogeneous communities, nobody will demand that you convert. It's merely another issue of small-town conformity. A majority of people in town share a set of beliefs—in this case, about how and where to conduct their spiritual lives.

If these traditions happen to coincide with yours—if worshipping with others is already part of your routine—your adjustment to your new life may be easier. You'll meet people in church, participate in church social activities and committees and establish a base from which to extend your social presence in town. If your traditions differ, you won't necessarily be shunned, at least consciously. But it may take you longer to meet people and "get in the swing of things" because you don't share this important part of your neighbors' lives.

10. Filled with characters

If you move to a small town, will everyone you meet be as kooky as the characters in a William Faulkner novel or an episode of TV's *Northern Exposure*?

The percentage of nutty individuals in a small town probably isn't much different from that in the city. It may be, however, that the characters are more visible in the small town. With the smaller community, you're apt to form a more personal relationship with everybody you meet, both your straight-arrow neighbors and the fellow who mumbles to himself at the train station. Because there's only one set of stores, you may keep running into local ne'er-do-wells whom you would have more easily dismissed or avoided in the city.

It may seem like there are more characters in a small town because residents are more aware of everyone's idiosyncrasies. The lack of secrets in a small town means that everyone knows what old Mr. Withers did during the war. In the city, you could have lived next door to Mr. Withers without knowing the background that makes him such a character. A slight nonconformity can be much more evident in a small town. (And of course, your own nonconformities based on your habituation to city life will make you a real character, too.)

Popular culture: The Englishman...

The movie *The Englishman Who Went Up a Hill but Came Down a Mountain* (made in 1995) places Hugh Grant in the middle of a town full of goofy people. Although it's set in Wales, there are some instructive parallels to America.

Grant plays a World War I-era surveyor charged with measuring the height of an unpronounceable geographic feature. If it's less than 1,000 feet high, it will be classified as a "hill," despite the fact that everyone in town proudly refers to it as "the mountain." This parochialism is typical of small towns, which often boast about historical happenings, native-born celebrities or annual events that nobody from more than 50 miles away has ever heard of or cared about.

In the movie, after an initial survey suggests the mountain will not qualify, the town pulls together to build it high enough to be a mountain, meanwhile distracting Grant and his supervisor long enough to pull off the stunt. Again, the pulling together for civic duty (silly as that duty may seem to outsiders) is a hallmark of tightly knit small towns. The effort is led by an austere minister, Reverend Jones, and a fun-loving innkeeper, Morgan. These two despise each other and everything the other represents but are still quite civil. Though the narrator describes them as never talking to each other, they do in fact greet each other on the street. And in the time of crisis, they pull together for the common need.

The supervisor finds small-town life boring. A clotheshorse who dismisses the locals as unsophisticated rubes, he locks himself in his room with a bottle of gin. Obviously, he would not a be good candidate to move to a small town.

Grant's character, while liking the town very much, is aware that despite (or perhaps because of) his education, he's really not qualified for any local career. However, when he and the young woman the town enlisted to "distract" him fall in love, he decides to move there. Like many movies, this one portrays only this decision and not its aftermath. Starting his new life—while hardly as dramatic—may prove an equally challenging task.

Additionally, there's typically less fear associated with nonconformity in a small town. Everyone knows Troy, everyone knows he's weird, and everyone knows he's harmless. He's lived here all his life and nothing's ever come of it. In the city, without that knowledge, unusual behavior can have a dark side. Recently, near my parent's home in an upscale Eastern suburb, we encountered a naked man cross-country skiing through a park in June. (He was using dry-land cross-country ski training equipment.) Our amusement was tinged with concern: Would this park be safe for a single female? With the rumor mill in a small town, he'd quickly become known—possibly arrested or forced out of town, but possibly tolerated and approved as safe. We typically fear the unknown; in a small town, for better or worse, everything is known.

11. Agrarian and self-sufficient

Don't assume that small towns will be full of fresh produce or any of the other benefits (or drawbacks) of agricultural dependence. Only three percent of the national population works in the agricultural sector, which means that many people far from cities are nevertheless far from farmers.

So if your vision of the small town is a place dominated by agriculture, keep in mind that some small towns are not. Obviously, farms comprise the largest part of the economy of many small towns, particularly in the Great Plains. But other small towns are dominated by logging, mining, fishing, tourism or a local manufacturing facility. In fact, according to Philip Burgess of the Center for the New West, a Denver think tank, less than a quarter of the nation's 2,400 rural counties are predominately agriculture. And the small town economic base continues to diversify. For example, Burgess notes that 40 percent of the new jobs from 1988 to 1990 in South Dakota were in manufacturing.

In terms of your lifestyle, locally grown products are likely to become somewhat more important, though not overwhelmingly so. It's easier to have a garden in a small town than in the city. You may have a larger lot than an urban resident, and the air and water are cleaner. Gardening is also the sort of slow-paced outdoor activity that small town residents, as opposed to harried suburbanites, are more likely to enjoy.

But one can't extend this generalization too far. If you want to work with the earth as a commercial enterprise, rather than a personal hobby, be ready for a lot of work. As we approach the 21st century, we also approach the near-extinction of the successful independent family farm. Many productive farms have consolidated into "agribusiness" enterprises. And while a few hardworking, creative souls continue at the family level, most are forced to rely on outside sources of income—either another job or a large savings account—to make ends meet. Farming is a demanding business, requiring the intelligence and training to choose and plan wisely, yet also the patience to perform repetitive, often tedious tasks on a daily basis. It also requires long, long hours—which may take you away from the community life you were striving for in moving out of the city.

Between machinery and fertilizers, agriculture has also become a tremendously capital-intensive industry, further hampered by low margins and considerable risks. This traditionally conservative industry may also face confusing and strenuous times as government subsidies continue to dwindle.

12. Backward

Some urban folks make the mistake of confusing education and access to culture with brains. Though you won't necessarily be surrounded by prize-winning physicists and poets, most small-town people are hardly the rubes you might think.

"We each had the typical urban prejudices about folks living in 'the sticks'—that they're narrow-minded, inbred and so on," says Charlie Mitchell, who lives in a rural area outside of Elmira, N.Y. "But we were wrong." And Mitchell is a good judge of intelligence and sophistication: He's chair of the American Studies department at Elmira College. Before moving to upstate New York, he and his wife had been in academic communities at Yale University and the College of William and Mary.

In Peterborough, N.H., Tom Forman hooked up with a local chapter of the Anthroposophical Society, a group of people interested in a certain view of the world. (The society's intellectual beliefs are so complex as to defy summarization here.) "The chapter here is stronger and healthier than the one in the Boston area," Forman says. He finds Peterborough a stimulating place—quite far from anti-intellectual. "I'm translating books on a variety of subjects from German. I'm able to get involved in this community doing things that interest me. It's a happy situation."

Many small-town residents are extremely intelligent—just in different ways than you may be used to. They may not have had a college education, but instead began operating a small business soon after high school. (Running a small business can be a challenging intellectual adventure and a great education.) Others may have a college degree (or more than one) but "dropped out" of the mainstream for one reason or another. Perhaps they decided they didn't like working in an office...or never intended to. They simply pursued a degree in English or art to get more out of their spare time. For example, Tracy Kidder's book *House* profiled Apple Corps, a group of carpenters based in a tiny Berkshire town. Two of the four carpenters had college degrees, one of them from Dartmouth.

These long-term, small-town residents are currently being augmented by an influx of educated, sophisticated people. You may be among this crowd. The "ACWs" (the acronym refers to technocommuters and stands for Another Computer in the Woods) bring a mix of skills and backgrounds to many rural communities. As Lisa Rogak writes in her move-to-the-country newsletter *Sticks*, "In most rural areas, there are many intelligent, highly trained people who moved to the country because their happiness was more important than what they did for a living or how much money they made. Ironically, the further out you get, the truer this is."

Rogak hints at an important difference: These educated people may have very different interests than their urban counterparts. They may pay very little attention to issues of fashion, culture, modern convenience or new ways to make money. And they probably see this lifestyle as far more "intelligent" than the urban one. For example, though they know Shakespeare, they may prefer to talk about horses. Though they followed a Presidential campaign 20 years ago, they may have decided national politics are a waste of time. You may not get into the same types of conversations you did in the city, but by asking the right questions, you may learn a great deal.

In fact, it may be you who has to do the catching up to avoid looking and acting stupid. "Growing up in New York City and Newark, N.J.," says Karen Good of Rockport, Maine, "I never had to learn about burning wood, how oil furnaces worked or how to keep a garden—things I need to live here successfully. But certainly this is a place full of human beings, just like anywhere else."

13. Clean

Small towns have the popular image of being clean and free of pollution. In general, the impression is correct. On the other hand, small towns sometimes have varying, unique types of pollution problems.

Moving to some small towns can actually bring you closer to some forms of pollution. Hazardous waste dumps and nuclear power plants, for example, are usually located away from population centers. Small towns often don't have the political clout to stop them—some even encourage them, desiring the jobs they provide.

Other small towns house industries such as oil refineries, wood processing plants, mines or quarries. While many operate in an environmentally friendly manner, their existence (or the remnants of their past existence) can still mean that air and/or water quality is not all you would hope for.

The odor of small town life is not always of flowers and freshly mowed grass. In addition to industrial plants, a small town might have rendering plants, sugar beet harvesting facilities and/or slaughterhouses. Other sources of odor can include paper mills, seafood processing facilities or a poorly designed septic system at a tourist resort. Cow manure is the classic scent of country living, but some people who have never been exposed to it may find they'd rather move back to the city and aromas with which they are more familiar.

Litter in a small town may simply be larger than that in the city. Instead of discarded fast-food packaging, there are rusted-out appliances and junked cars. Recently, rural West Virginia has tried to clean up its image as a place whose scenic beauty is overwhelmed by the detritus of human habitation. The state is perhaps unfairly singled out: The roadsides and mountaintops of many rural communities are littered with wastes from households and corporations that didn't care enough about the future appearance of their community.

Small towns are heralded for good water quality, where the tap water tastes good enough to drink. Again, however, the general rule has frequent exceptions. Try some. (As an urbanite accustomed to bottled water, you might overlook the water dispenser in a Realtor's office. But its presence may mean that the local water supply isn't much better than the one you're trying to escape.) Even in the most remote wilderness areas, the days of drinking straight from a mountain stream may be gone forever. The presence of giardia—a nasty virus producing recurring diarrhea-like symptoms—causes many savvy mountaineers to drink absolutely nothing that hasn't been boiled, treated or filtered first.

Despite this myriad of warnings, you can expect a healthier, cleaner environment in most small towns. Many small-town residents cite air and water quality as some of the most important factors in their decision to live where they do.

14. Quiet

Many people consider noise a form of pollution, and again, the small town is cleaner than an urban downtown. You may hear a siren once a month rather than once an hour.

However, the small town comes with its own forms of noise. Rural recreation often involves chain saws, motorboats or snowmobiles, any of which can shatter the "peace" you were seeking (especially if you're seeking it on a sailboat or cross-country skis). To take advantage of fickle weather conditions, many farmers must run their tractors very late at night. And that wonderful symbol of rural life—the rooster crowing at dawn—may not be all that welcome if, unlike the rooster or farmer, you prefer to sleep past 5:30 a.m.

Once every few years, we get another media report of somebody who moved to the country and then sued a neighbor in protest of the noise or pollution that are byproducts of agricultural life. The judgments invariably favor the farmers, who have the benefit of longevity (as well as common sense) on their side. So if you want quiet, look—and listen—carefully to the *type* of quiet you'll get in your new home.

15. Cheap

Our final category is one of the most important for many people: Isn't it a lot cheaper to live in a small town? Lowering your cost of living may be one of your primary motivations in considering moving to a small town. You may have skipped immediately to this section, not giving a hoot about some of the other alleged "benefits" of small-town life. If so, there's good news, although not good enough to allow you to stop reading just yet.

The perception is generally accurate. Small towns are cheaper to live in than more metropolitan areas. However, you generally *make* much less money in a small town. If you're retired, being transferred by a large corporation or you've got your own business that depends on out-of-state clientele, then you may not need to worry. Otherwise, you do need to worry.

Let's be blunt: You don't just make a little less money, you make a lot less money. In 1992, the Job Service in Kalispell, Mont., reported hearing from a bank president who was desperate to leave California. "I'll even take a 50 percent pay cut," he said. So they asked him how much he made. He said, "Three hundred thousand dollars a year."

The response was laughter and amazement. Banking jobs at $150,000 a year didn't even exist in Montana, much less with vacancies. In fact, so many educated people were pouring into Kalispell looking for employment at the time, the fellow might have been lucky to find a $5-an-hour teller job.

High-paying jobs don't exist. And low-paying jobs are really low. Do any of your contemporaries work for minimum wage? It's not uncommon in a small town. In fact, most small-town jobs pay minimum wage. Waitresses, bartenders, household help, agricultural laborers and retail clerks often earn less than $5 per hour.

It may be a long time since you worked for minimum wage. It's worth some thought: At $5 an hour, working a full eight-hour day, you make $40. Before taxes. That's $200 a week, less than $1,000 a month. Even if moving to a small town got your housing costs below $500 a month, those costs could still take up more than half your income. Are you really ready for such a change?

In particular, tourist resorts are notorious for paying low wages and not offering benefits, especially for seasonal employees. That last vacation spot that you absolutely loved may have an abnormally high ratio of low-paying, service-sector positions. Burger flippers, motel chambermaids, gift-shop assistants—all work at minimum wage. There's no pay when you don't work—even if you're sick. If you want insurance, you have to buy it yourself. It's a wonderfully romantic notion to live in a mountain or beach resort—but you may end up infuriated by the day-to-day drag of slaving away for little reward so that others can have their fun.

The cost of living is driven by the cost of housing. It's cheaper to live in a small town because housing costs are cheaper. Land is cheaper because there's more of it. And in the heartland, housing is especially available because small-town population has dwindled and aged.

How much cheaper varies by the town and region. Some chic resorts have housing costs as high as those in the city (although costs are often not as high as they would be in the correspondingly chic neighborhood in the city). Karen Connelly found that housing prices in Jackson Hole were roughly comparable to those in Washington, D.C. Robyn Kratzer found that Park City, Utah, was 50 percent more expensive than Houston.

Keep in mind that housing costs may include more than mortgage or rent. You may also want to consider utilities, taxes and other ancillary costs. You may hope to cut your heating bill by moving to a warmer climate—but the costs of air conditioning may be more than the costs of heat. Unlike more populated locations, your preferred method of heating may not be available. And what's available, such as propane or electric heat, may prove exceedingly expensive. Tom Forman was pleased to hear that his new house in Peterborough, N.H., used gas. Then, when he moved in, he discovered that it was propane gas rather than the inexpensive natural gas he'd expected.

You'll need to do some research as to how much moving to a specific small town could lower your housing costs. You'll also have to research how much lowering your housing costs would lower your cost of living. What percentage of your income do you spend on housing? Remember that other items—food, automobiles, clothing and luxury items, for example—may cost more in the small town, reflecting higher transportation costs and lower economies of scale with the remote location. (If you travel a lot for business or pleasure, the remote location may increase those costs for you as well.) If a large portion of your budget goes to these "other" expenditures, lowering your housing costs may not make much of a change in the overall picture. Likewise, if you're currently feeling the pinch from automobile, medical or credit-card loans, even a 40 percent reduction in your rent or mortgage payment may not be enough to help you, especially if it's accompanied by a matching or larger reduction in income.

Another factor that keeps down the cost of living in a small town is not reflected in any mathematical calculation. It's also something that may not necessarily work in your favor. In a small town, there's nothing to spend money on.

In the city, you may find your paycheck dwindling more rapidly than you'd like simply because you are so active. You go out to dinner, see a show, attend a lecture, do a little shopping downtown, take some classes, go to a concert, etc. In the small town, as we discussed earlier, many of these options may not be available. It's an old-fashioned good-news/bad-news joke: The good news is, the movie tickets cost only $4; the bad news is, all the movies are six months old. (Meanwhile, if you have to drive 100 miles to get to a "decent" theater, factoring in gas and time starts making movies *really* expensive.) The good news is, classes at the community college have just a nominal fee; the bad news is, the only classes are in agricultural economics. The good news is, there's no cover charge at the bar; the bad news is, the band knows only three songs.

Though the *supply* of housing in rural areas can keep housing costs low, these costs are also influenced by *demand*. Simply put, places get expensive to live in when they're desirable. The most frequent factor influencing housing costs is access to good jobs. Housing costs can also be influenced by scenery, shopping, accessibility and safety. In short, many of the factors that make you want to live there make others want to live there, too. If you want cheap housing costs, you may have to put up with being "in the middle of nowhere." If you want a lot of amenities, you may have to pay more for them. Some lucky folks find both, but such opportunities may be fleeting. If you return to the same town five years later, property values may be out of reach.

C. How well do they fit?

We've talked about what you want and what small towns offer. Now it's time to put them together: Do the two correspond at all?

Presumably you've been answering this question as you've been reading. If not, you might want to pause at this point and go over the last section. With each description of small town life, ask *Is this what I want? Can I be happy with this?*

1. Your intuition—better than a model

Some books suggest that you can arrive at an answer to whether small-town life works for you by setting up a rigorous analysis. Some even devise quantitative models, assigning numeric values to various factors—or asking you to assign your own.

There's a much simpler way to determine whether you should move to a small town. It's not necessarily easier to perform, but it's certainly easier to explain. And it's guaranteed to be true to your inner self. It's this: Trust your intuition. A good test will reveal aspects of your personality, but those same aspects are revealed by choices you make when you trust your intuition.

It's not easy to trust your intuition. First you have to recognize what it is:

- What is the real you speaking, and what are the expectations of your family, friends or co-workers?

- Which dreams are things you really want to accomplish, and which are simply temporary escapes from an otherwise happy situation?

- Which fears represent your sense of how you would really fit in these new surroundings, and which are meaningless neuroses?

Sorting through these questions and your answers can take some hard (but valuable) thought.

The second difficult task is obeying your intuition. Your family, friends and co-workers may try to argue you out of your position. And your only response is, "But it feels right." The difficulty comes in being satisfied that you don't need any more reason than that. Here's a hint: Look at the past important decisions in your life, such as going to college, choosing a career or getting married. Did you make them based on an intuitive sense of what would work for you? And was that intuition correct? The more experience we have with our intuition, the more comfortable we are trusting it.

Many people I interviewed for this book said they knew they'd made the right decision because the place they were moving *felt like home.* They could extol scenery or friendliness or pace, but in the end it came down to this intuitive sense of how they fit into the community, how the community touched on and responded to their conceptions of a place they would consider "home." For example, Mary Beasley said that soon after she moved to Oxford, Miss., "It feels like coming home." And in discussing her move from New Jersey to rural Maine, Karen Good says, "I've never regretted it. It was like coming home."

2. Some exercises

Still having trouble making the decision? Consider some of the following tricks:

1. **Write a letter to a friend.** You often write what you think. Since writing takes more time than talking, you get a chance to poke around your thoughts.

2. **If you keep a diary, try to convince the diary that you should move.** Then try to convince the diary you should stay. If you haven't traditionally kept a diary, consider starting one to keep track of your thoughts on this subject. If you do keep a diary, look back at previous entries—is moving to a small town a fleeting notion or something you've been interested in for a while?

3. **Write a letter to your spouse or significant other explaining why the two of you should move.** This is a letter you won't mail—because your spouse is right there to talk to—but by using different media (writing and talking) you may find yourself exploring different arguments.

4. **Make a list of all the reasons you should move.** On another sheet of paper, list all the reasons to stay. For each reason, evaluate how *important* it is and how *likely* it is. For example, you may not want to move to a small town because you fear being eaten by a grizzly bear—something you decide is not too likely but nevertheless very important. Never compare simply the lengths of each list; instead look at the items you weigh heavily in each category.

5. **Test drive your decision.** Spend a week with the attitude that you're going to move next month. Then spend a week with the attitude that moving is a silly dream— you're going to give it up and be happier living your life the way it is. You may want to keep a diary during these two weeks, or at least jot down some emotions on the back of an envelope. At the end of the two-week period, look back: Which way were you happier? Which caused less anxiety, more peace? Did either attitude cause you to be more effective in your job or your relationship?

6. **Flip a coin.** Heads you move, tails you stay. You can only do this once, because you're going to abide by the decision of the coin. When you flip it, send it high in the air. While it's in the air, you'll realize how you hope it'll land. You'll be rooting for either heads or tails. There's your decision. That's what you want, your intuition speaking. Obey it. You won't even need to look at the coin.

3. Tradeoffs

Choosing to move to a small town—like any choice—involves numerous tradeoffs. You can't have everything you want; you need to decide which end of the tradeoff is more important.

Do you want nature or capitalism? In *Edge City*, Joel Garreau notes that mankind's early history was tied to nature (such as agriculture and hunting); city life has been tied to capitalism (such as new products and challenging careers). In modern times, we're always seeking to bridge the two. Suburbs are an attempt to bring aspects of nature (in the form of trees and grass) to the city. "Edge cities" (Garreau's term for the mall-and-office-park culture that is springing up on beltways and near airports) are an attempt to bring aspects of capitalism to the country. Neither is entirely successful. But nothing will completely, successfully bridge that gap: We need to decide which side of the bridge we prefer.

Do you want community or independence? To some extent this is the same tradeoff. Nature depends on a web of interconnected communities (for example, ants working together to build a colony). The small town is much more successful at retaining that sense of, as Lawrence

Haworth wrote in *The Good City*, "living a common life and having common concerns." On the other hand, the specialization and diversity of urban life allows you to be more of an individual, to fully express yourself without worrying about how others will react.

Some of us love the small town because it delineates our aspirations (simplicity, generosity or connectedness), which are made all the more clear by their stark opposition to our current existence (greedy, thoughtless or manipulative). We like small towns as philosophy. As theory. But we wouldn't want to *live* in one.

What we seek is a paradox. For example, we want a home that's:

Rural..................	but...sophisticated
Crime-free...........	but...wealthy
Stress-free...........	but...stimulating
Quiet..................	but...vibrant
Relaxed...............	but...busy
Communal...........	but...independent
Safe....................	but...adventurous
Rustic.................	but...comfortable
Historic...............	but...contemporary
Traditional..........	but...innovative
Consistent...........	but...trendy
Rugged...............	but...refined
Simple.................	but...stylish
Parochial.............	but...worldly

This is what all of us seek in life—a proper balance. Many people who are dissatisfied with their urban homes feel that things have gotten too out of balance. Life is too stressful, too violent or not quiet or communal enough. A little bit was manageable, when it was balanced, but now it's gotten out of whack.

Yet this lack of balance is the same reason many people are dissatisfied with small-town life. It's too quiet, too staid, not sophisticated or comfortable enough. A little bit would be manageable, if it was balanced, but this community is out of whack.

How long does this take?

How long does it take to decide to move to a small town? With all of our discussion about the decision process, you may be worried that you can't make a spur-of-the-moment decision—or that you can't dilly-dally.

Of course the answer depends on the individual. In his studies of people who moved to Montana, sociologist Pat Jobes found that one in 10 had made a snap decision, and one in 10 had thought about it for five years or more. The rest were somewhere in between.

How long does it take? It takes long enough for you to feel comfortable with the decision. If you're still waffling, then you may not be ready. If you absolutely love your job and your company doesn't have a telecommuting option, then you may not be ready. If you're waiting for a gourmet coffee shop to open in town, then you may not be ready. (Once the coffee shop opens, you'll wait for a nice bookstore. You'll invent excuses until property values shoot out of your reach.)

You'll be ready when you feel comfortable with these tradeoffs. When answers occur to you as quickly as the questions do—and you're comfortable with the answers. When you can say, "I'll get my own espresso maker" or "I'll find another great job" or "I like my life, but it's time for a change."

Remember that the decision to move is not the end product. Starting your new life will take a lot of energy. It'll take time, commitment and strength of character. When you're ready to take on this challenge—when you're looking forward to it, even—then you're ready to move. As long as you're considering the *decision* to move as a solution to your woes, you're not ready. Once you start looking at the decision to move as the first step in your new life, then you have in effect arrived.

How out of balance are you? What will it take to balance you out? A new volunteer position? A new ability to say no? Tighter security in your home? Or a drastic change in your lifestyle?

Be careful that you don't run from one end of the spectrum to the other. Realize that we're all somewhere in the middle of this paradox—we always will be. No single place can match all of our desires. It's just a matter of determining which ones are most important.

Do you want safety and environmental purity or do you want convenience and diversity? The convenience of a mall around the corner will, inescapably, take away from your scenic view. The safety of a close-knit community may shun outsiders (perhaps based on unfair stereotypes). The "convenience" (some might call it a necessity) of a regular paycheck at the local sawmill may contaminate the environmental purity of your drinking water.

Do you want a lack of stimulation or stress? After all, stress is a product of too much stimulation—career, family and extracurricular activities all demanding too much of your time. Getting the proper amount of stimulation is a delicate balance and one that can be easily upset. In the city, you're used to refusing things because they'd contribute to stress; in the small town, you may need to search them out so as to avoid boredom. Is that change in outlook something you can bring about in yourself?

20 Questions:
How does this sound?

These are some attributes of small-town life. For each one, ask: Is this desirable? If so, how *important* is it?

1. Everybody knows a lot about you—even people you've never met.

2. As a rule, inexpensive real estate brings a lower cost of living. But you *make* a lot less money, too.

3. There's nowhere to shop, so most people don't shop much.

4. An individual's intelligence may be expressed in ways you're not familiar with.

5. Everyone nods at you or greets you on the street.

6. The community has a firm idea of its goals and values...and uneasiness with people who seem not to share them.

7. A "good" restaurant features simple (rather than "interesting") food and friendly (rather than "professional") service.

8. People spend a great deal of time outdoors.

9. People regularly stop to chat with each other.

10. Things don't get done when you thought they would.

11. The few cultural events are generally of lesser "quality."

12. Threats to your safety from other humans (such as a robbery, burglary or random shooting) are far less, though threats from other sources (Mother Nature) may still exist.

13. The strength of tradition produces a great sense of history...but great reluctance to innovation.

14. Very few people dress up. Ever.

15. People often participate in entertainment rather than consuming it.

16. People recognize and wave at your car.

17. The area is clean and quiet, though those terms may be defined differently than you're used to.

18. Many (though not all) people include church activities as part of their spiritual, intellectual and social lives.

19. People love gardening, though as a hobby rather than an income source.

20. Many people marry young.

Chapter 2

Evaluating a small town

Which *small town is right for me?*

Let's say you've decided to move to a small town. You think you'll fit in well in a tight-knit community; the slow-paced lifestyle appeals to you. But which place is right for your interests and needs?

This chapter serves two purposes:

- If you need help choosing a destination, this chapter examines some ways to *identify* and rank candidates.

- If you already have a destination (or a very short list of destinations) in mind, this chapter helps you *evaluate* whether a given small town is a good one.

The popularity of books that rate places to live suggests that many of you fall in the first camp. You want to leave the city but are unsure how to do so or where to go. Yet my experience suggests that many of you are in the second camp: You have an opportunity to move to a specific small town because of a job, family or friends. And you want to know whether this small town will be a good one. In fact, determining the quality of this specific destination may help determine whether you leave the city at all.

This chapter will address both concerns and:

• Ways to identify potential small towns you might want to move to.

• Factors that make small towns successful.

• Acquiring the information you need to evaluate a small town.

• A big secret: the nearly guaranteed predictor of your future comfort level in a small town.

Thus, if you already have a town in mind, you might be able to skip to Section 2B.

A. Choosing a small town

1. A big task: determining differences among towns

With 128,000 distinct "places" (as defined by the Census Bureau) spread over 3.5 million square miles, the United States offers a daunting number of small towns to which you can move.

As mentioned in the Introduction, there's no question that there are similarities in small towns across the country. Americans' mobility, plus the standardization of mass entertainment, has brought a general national character to small towns in almost every nook and cranny of the country.

Indeed, a book called *The Clustering of America* by Michael Weiss argues that the nation can be broken into 40 neighborhood types. For example, Weiss argues that Princeton, N.J., and Palo Alto, Calif., are more similar to each other than they are to the communities that surround them geographically. (Both house well-known universities, which have helped to establish high-tech industries and upper-class residential neighborhoods.)

Weiss's chief measure of comparison is consumer preferences. That is, people in neighborhood types are found to be "similar" because they have preferences for similar consumer items—everything from magazines to microwaves. This focus on consumer preferences mirrors the real-world use of this theory: Marketers use ZIP codes to help predict neighborhoods in which their products might sell well. His analysis suggests that small towns are as easily categorized as the consumer items he uses to study them.

On the other hand, one of the things we value about small towns is their uniqueness. "That place has character," we like to say. Though difficult to define, such character is often a product of physical setting, history, architecture, economics and other factors that set this town off from "faceless suburbs" or even the unique, character-filled towns surrounding it.

As independent, autonomous economic units, most small towns have a variety of consumers. One neighborhood may contain both the owner and employees of retail business; both the principal and janitor at the school. The ZIP-code marketers can't be as sure of their audience. Many people who enjoy living in small towns appreciate this sense in which they are difficult to pigeonhole.

Also, small towns typically value history and tradition. Many residents have lived there for many years, perhaps all their lives. Sometimes, as Tom Forman found in Peterborough, N.H., the town seems unchanged in 50 years. Metropolitan areas, on the other hand, frequently focus on the future rather than the past. They point with pride at their skyscrapers rather than their cemeteries. People are also more likely to move in and out of metropolitan areas (or around to different neighborhoods within an area), loosening those links with the past. The focus on tradition allows small towns to retain a greater sense of their regional or local heritage.

The bad economic times so many small towns have encountered have also helped preserve unique local cultures. As they've lost residents to cities through this century, small towns have retained an "historic" look by default. The historic architecture you admire might well have been renovated beyond recognition or even torn down if anyone had possessed enough money to do so. Had the small town market been bigger, it would have caused new construction—which would have been in the form of homogenized malls and strips, just like the suburbs. It wasn't any sense of higher moral character that prevented architectural despoliation of small towns, it was lack of cash. Indeed, the Wal-Mart phenomenon, despite its critics, simply offers rural residents the opportunities for cheap prices in a mall setting—opportunities for which metropolitan residents have time and again demonstrated their preference. In short, "quaint" often corresponds with "poor." The economic misfortune of the small town has been to the benefit of those who value its unique history and culture.

One of the most hopeful trends in contemporary small towns is that "uniqueness" and "quality" seem to go hand in hand. (I use "seem to" because uniqueness and quality are both vague terms that can vary considerably across individuals.) In *The 100 Best Small Towns in America*, Norman Crampton measured quality using a complicated formula involving population, average income, percentage of nonwhites, percentage of 25- to 34-year-olds, number of physicians per capita, number of serious crimes per capita, percentage of college-educated individuals (which he used to gauge employment opportunities), local government spending on education, and the presence of or proximity to a county seat, daily newspaper, institution of higher learning, designated "scenic" area and nearby metropolitan area.

Many towns that scored highly in Crampton's quality rankings are also unique. For example, the port town of Beaufort, S.C., has a rich cultural and social heritage, as well as architecture, that has led it to be the setting for several movies. Williamstown, Mass., has a unique focus on education and the arts, with more art museums and theater performances per capita than perhaps anywhere else in the country. Bisbee, Ariz., is an old copper-mining town with a turn-of-the-century air that gives it an almost European flavor. Yet none of these qualities were explicitly measured by Crampton's formula.

In short, though Crampton doesn't say this, his book suggests that not only do small towns differ, but good small towns differ more. Because people are attracted to the unique cultural, social or historical aspects of these towns, they will then work at creating income, bringing in doctors, spending money on education and the other factors that Crampton used to judge quality.

While celebrating these differences, this book will not delve into them. I certainly recommend that you investigate unique towns, but you must define "unique" for yourself. Perhaps your unique town has been shaped by fishing, mountain biking, Cajun cooking, coal mining, the Mormon religion or flinty New England spirit. I believe such uniqueness often correlates with the best-functioning communities in the country. But only you can decide what works for you.

2. Not so big a task: working on your criteria

Choosing a small town may actually be a lot easier than you might expect. As mentioned above, many people who actually move to small towns did *not* spend a lot of time thinking about the choice. Most people who are happy in their small town do not look back and see the choice as difficult. They rarely ask if they could have chosen a different place. Some don't stay in their initial choice, moving on (often nearby) due to factors related to employment, housing or additional knowledge they've gained about the area after having lived there a while. But typically, looking back, they say they knew this region was "right."

Choosing a location: Bob Renner

"Our choice was based mostly on economics," says Bob Renner of Coos Bay, Ore. Bob and his wife hoped to leave the San Francisco Bay area when he retired from Sears. "We enjoy the coast," he says. "Monterey and Big Sur were out of our range. As you move north up the coast, prices start going down, but it's still fairly pricey. The central coast of Oregon still has excellent opportunities for retirement homes," he says.

The Renners bought their home two years before Bob's retirement and rented it out. Visiting every four to six months, they made some contacts with their new neighbors. "We savored the thought of leaving the Bay Area," he says. "And yet when we would visit Coos Bay, we would turn on the radio and hear the 'bay area weather.' That helped us feel like we belonged here, by trading bay areas."

The Renners moved three months before Bob retired, and he commuted to Fremont, working two or three weeks at a time and then spending a week in Oregon. "Any move in conjunction with a major life change could be traumatic," he says. "But it was fine for us."

Like many migrants, he cites an improved "quality of life" in the small town. He elaborates: "The air quality is better. It's quieter. Kids still have boom boxes, but you can't hear them a half-mile away. There are fewer signs of crime and violence, such as graffiti or vandalism. It happens, but isn't paraded in front of you. Beach access is simpler, less crowded. But clean air is the big difference. When you return to the hideous rat race, that rush-hour traffic, it makes you glad to have a new home. It's a sad commentary on the city but unfortunately very real."

When the choice of which town you want to live in is easy, the decision to move there becomes easier as well. In my case, after just three hours in my current town, I knew I wanted to move here. When I arrived in town, I had no expectation of moving. But after experiencing the place, I had no desire to continue living in the city.

Looking back, I realized that the decision to move to a small town had not sprung fully formed on that day. In the previous five years, I'd contemplated moving to towns in the Berkshires, Cape Cod, Florida and Washington state. But I had a hard time choosing among them, so I never followed through on any of them. When the choice was easy, so was the execution.

Thus, though we've put them in different chapters of this book, there may well be some overlap between your decision to move to a small town and your evaluation of a specific town or towns.

3. Identifying candidates

Still worried about the difficulty of finding your small town? Let me show you how easy it is. You must fall into at least one of the following four camps:

1. You or your spouse has been offered a **job** in a specific small town.

2. You have **family** or friends in a specific small town, or perhaps two or three.

3. You visited an area, fell in **love** with it and have decided you absolutely have to live there.

4. You have specific **geographic criteria**, such as proximity to a beach or a river with Class IV whitewater.

If you're moving for a job (**Case #1**), there's not much involved in choosing a small town—it's where the job is. Deciding whether to take the job and move there is difficult, but at least you don't have the problem of choosing the town from scratch.

Likewise with **Case #2**: The small town you're selecting is where your family connections are (though this may bring special concerns, which are addressed in the next section).

Case #3 is the most interesting—and the riskiest. People in this category derive great satisfaction from a sense of place and are willing to take chances to capture that satisfaction. These types of people are the most interesting participants in the "why-you-came" game—a popular topic of conversation in growing small towns. How did you get here? What factors brought you to town? How did you choose this place? For these people, the story of the move is the story of their lives. They tell it with passion and pride. (However, it's not necessarily unique, as jaded long timers will sometimes point out.)

In the end, though, there's not much advice to offer in the area of falling in love with a small town. Like falling in love with a person, it's a complex and very personal emotional reaction. Maybe it's already happened to you, maybe it will happen to you or maybe you fall into **Case #4**, where you'll actively investigate potential solutions.

Are you looking for a specific type of weather? A mode of recreation? Regional culture? Proximity to a certain city or natural feature? In Chapter 1, you spent some time defining exactly what it is you want. The purpose of that task wasn't just to focus on whether small town life would work for you: Those criteria will also quickly narrow your list of candidate towns.

For example, you may decide that you want to live in the South, be within 120 miles of a major metropolis with an airport hub and live in a mountainous region which has milder summer weather. So you're able to limit your search to the southern Appalachians in Georgia, Tennessee and North Carolina (with access to Atlanta or possibly Charlotte). Another example: Family is important to you, and an aunt lives in Topeka, Kan., and cousins in Madison, Wis. You want small town flavor and a strong manufacturing economy to provide for your career. Again, the search is going to be quite limited. Spend some time with a commercial atlas (which provides census data on economics and demographics, as well as maps), and you can come up with some candidates fairly quickly. (See the Appendix for recommendations on atlases and other resources discussed in this section.)

Specialized associations or magazines can also provide helpful information. Where are golf courses open (and conditions playable) year-round? Where are vibrant square-dancing groups? Where are great places to go bird-watching? Identify an enthusiasts' group or trade association for your interest and call or write them with questions like these.

They may even be able to point you toward specific towns offering the amenities you're interested in.

Depending on your criteria, you may find that much of this research has already been done for you. It may have been compiled, quantified and/or rated in a category of books and multimedia materials I'll refer to as "ratings books."

Every month, it seems, a new ratings book is published. The books differ in focus, quality and usefulness. But nobody can deny that the genre is popular. And why not? Used effectively, a ratings book can save you time and headaches in suggesting places to live or providing data on those you're considering.

A good ratings book should be endlessly cross-referenced so you can look up your factors of interest. If you want to live in a town with a university, large manufacturing sector or highly rated golf course, you should be able to use an index to discover towns you might not have otherwise considered. The book should provide information on the job market, the quality of education and the cost of living. You should then be able to examine a wide variety of data on the town, such as age distribution, public transportation or weather, to allow you to move it up or down your personal list.

Ratings books are probably best at helping research a town you've already identified. They may confirm impressions you may have already gathered firsthand or from friends. Or more usefully, they may suggest areas you may want to research more on your own, by talking to people in the town. If you're looking to come up with ideas from scratch, however, these books may not be all that helpful. For a geography nut like me, the books are a lot of fun. I'm always interested in what a place is *like*, even when I'm trying to learn that information by just reading statistics or looking at maps. But I think the hobby is more entertaining than it is productive. For example, I knew from reading ratings books that I would like the climate in New Mexico or the Carolinas. I knew I'd like the number of bookstores in Berkeley, Calif., or Ann Arbor, Mich. I knew I'd like the number of musicians per capita in Austin, Texas. But such knowledge didn't prompt me to decide that I wanted to move to any of those places. What *did* make me decide to move was a personal connection I made with a place that—based on such statistics—I should have found too cold, remote and backward.

There's no doubt the books contain a wealth of data, especially for the "geographically illiterate." If you don't know exactly where Arkansas is or what the terrain, weather or economy is like there, such a book can help you out a great deal. If you've never heard of Elko, Nev., or Marshalltown, Iowa, reading such books can likewise provide background information on our country.

On the other hand, the books may be too statistics-laden for many people. (And many of the books resort to eye-catching but meaningless "Top 10"-type lists.) Furthermore, the statistics can sometimes be misleading. For example:

- **Be wary of books that forecast economic trends based on past data.** One ratings book, published in 1981, predicted that five of the top six income growth areas for the 1980s would be in Texas, and that New York City would be at the bottom of this list. This prediction correctly accounted for history: In the 70s, New York had struggled financially while Texas experienced an oil boom. Unfortunately it had the 80s exactly wrong. An oil bust decimated Texas, and the boom in financial services turned New York into a yuppie heaven.

- **Check that statistics—and even qualitative judgments—are not out of date.** A small town economy can go bust or real estate prices can shoot out of your reach in a matter of only two or three years. While some publishers are scrupulous about updating these books, your library may not have bought the most recent edition. You may want to double-check the statistics with a good bookstore or *Books in Print*.

- **Be wary of how data has been aggregated.** Because economic data on small towns can be paltry, some books may instead use data for a county or even a "nearby" metropolitan area. So all of the jobs in this supposedly booming location may be far from the specific town you're interested in—maybe even too far to commute.

Additionally, you'll need to carefully consider the value judgments and interpretations built into many of these data points. For example:

- **The unemployment rate is a good indicator of whether jobs are available, but not what *types* of jobs.** If all of the jobs available are as guards at the state prison and you don't want to do that, the low unemployment rate may not do you any good. You always have to keep in mind the small size of the market with which you are dealing. If you are an accountant moving to a town of 1,500 people that already has an accountant, there simply won't be enough work for you. Regardless of the unemployment rate, there is just not enough accounting to go around. It's for good reason that cowboys in the movies (who are, after all, small town people) always say, "This town ain't big enough for the both of us."

- **One book used the amount of money spent in restaurants as a gauge of entertainment options.** But if you love cheap barbecue shacks, your interests won't be captured. Another book used the number of stars in the restaurant ratings of a major guide book. This may be a better assessment of quality...assuming you agree with that guide book.

- **Statistics can accurately capture quantity without necessarily reflecting quality.** For example, there may be five square-dance callers in Jonesboro, but perhaps none of them are as good as the solitary one in Smithville. Jonesboro may have two mediocre hospitals, while Smithville may be the site of a regional center. Jonesboro may be closer to an airport—but it has fewer daily flights than Smithville to the places you want to go.

- **Do lots of hospital beds mean that a town has great health care or that there are a lot of sick people?** Does a high number of law enforcement officers mean the town is safe or that Sheriff Bubba has a lot of relatives who aren't suited for "regular" employment? In many cases, these books use the best data they can find for a given task. But because some things simply can't be quantified, that still may not be enough.

• **Your idea of quality may not agree with the authors'.**
For example, one book rates weather on mildness: A perfect
town would be 65 degrees year-round. Many of us, though,
prefer four seasons (even if one is quite harsh). And mild
climates are often rainy; many of us prefer sunshine and
would rate mild rainy towns at the bottom rather than the
top of the list. Most books are good about explicitly providing
their formulas, as well as the backup data, to allow you to
make your own judgments. But making those judgments
may still mean a lot of work for you.

Finally, as some of these books acknowledge, all of these "impar-
tial" criteria and statistics can't analyze the soul of a place and your
personal relationship to it. You'd never marry, sight unseen, a person
selected by a computer dating service; in fact, many of us don't believe
that a computer can do a better job than we can ourselves of identifying potential mates. Ratings books, with their complicated modeling and
dispassionate criteria, simulate computers. Their analyses and suggestions should be just a part of your overall strategy.

4. The value of relatives and friends

As you consider your move, the first towns that come to mind may
be ones in which you have friends or relatives. You've heard these people
talk about their communities, maybe you've visited them there. Maybe
you even spent part or all of your childhood at the family's country home.

Some people fear that there's something wrong with this. They
wonder if they shouldn't be more creative in coming up with a place to
live. On the contrary, however, places where you already know people
may make for the smoothest and easiest moves. In fact, if you haven't
yet, you might consider such a place.

If you haven't already, you might want to do an inventory of everyone you've ever known who has moved to a small town. (If you don't
think the list is long enough or want to be particularly thorough, ask
your friends to provide names of their small-town friends and relatives.) Write or call these old (or new) friends. Tell them of your plans,
ask for their impressions about their communities. Try to learn as
much as you can about their lives so that you can get as good a picture

as possible of what your life would be like in their shoes. As mentioned above, the personal connection will make these analyses much more real and vibrant to you than anything you could read in a book or a marketing brochure. These people's personal experiences in their towns will also probably be much more comprehensive than anything an author could pull together from census statistics or selected interviews.

The advantages of friends or family are obvious. They can introduce you to people, jobs, recreation sites, cultural events, local customs, dependable service people, useful retail outlets and countless other details of day-to-day life. They can be invaluable, particularly if you're shy or wary of trying new things yourself. How comforting to have someone you know you can turn to for answers, advice or introductions. (Sometimes it's nice to discover these things on your own. But even the most adventurous among us have periods where we want the security of some good recommendations.)

This is especially true for family, particularly in the South, where family is very much a social structure. Families gather on holidays, for Sunday dinners or for summer family reunions.

The customs, bonds and obligations of family are probably the strongest component of the "traditional American values" often associated with small towns. In a place and a lifestyle with fewer external pressures and activities, it's much easier for an entire family to sit down to dinner together every day. Where opportunities are more "wholesome" and less "cosmopolitan," it's easier to get everyone behind a family outing or event. In a community that's so small and tightly knit, it seems more natural to throw yourself behind school sporting events or activities. In a place that generally sees much less turnover than a city or suburb, regular gatherings of extended families seem all that more natural.

These impressions are not just nostalgia: There is empirical evidence. A Pennsylvania State University study found stronger family and social ties in country people.

If you feel close to your family or you would like to feel closer to them, these tendencies should work in your favor. There are, however, three caveats to keep in mind. One is that you may want to establish your own base when checking out a potential new home. In the book *Country Bound*, Marilyn and Tom Ross recommend avoiding social obligations and unsolicited opinions of friends and relatives, especially if you are condensing numerous activities into a tight schedule. The independence offered by a hotel room may well be worth the extra cost.

Second, if you move to a small town without any family nearby, you may occasionally feel left out. If the whole town attends the high school basketball game every Friday night, you may have nothing to do (unless, of course, you go along). When families gather for holidays, they may forget to include you. Meanwhile, there may be fewer single people to hang out with, particularly other single people without family connections. On Thanksgiving, all your friends may be back at the homestead.

The final (and perhaps most important) caveat is that a small town cannot "cure" a dysfunctional family. The reason your family spends little time together may be that it doesn't have time in a harried lifestyle—or it may be that you all just don't get along. In the last 20 years, our culture has come to a great awareness of the pitfalls of alcoholism, physical and sexual abuse and other dangerous patterns that often manifest themselves most harmfully in family situations. The fact that small towns often seem 20 years behind the times doesn't mean those problems don't exist there. Worse, what it means is that the support services to counteract those problems may not exist at adequate levels.

There can be a tremendous personal satisfaction in reconnecting with your roots—your family's traditional ways of doing things. If you come from five generations of Kentucky farmers, the patterns of rural Kentucky may be ingrained deep in your subconscious. The satisfaction you could gain out of returning to the family homestead may be a complicated internal psychological phenomenon or even one you may label as "spiritual." It may well fill a hole.

Of course it need not be a family home you're returning to. In fact, you may not be returning at all. If you grew up in a series of faceless suburbs, you may find that your "home" is hundreds or thousands of miles from where you were born. And you may find your "family" to be people not officially related to you, but sharing those spiritual values and quests.

Family burdens

In deciding to move to a place where you have family, consider:

- **Age difference.** Do you know people your age or just aunts and grandparents? A friend of mine spent her first six months in town living at the home of her 89-year-old grandmother. Her chief social outlet was Thursday lunch at the Senior Center. In finding a circle of contemporaries, she was faced with many of the same burdens as a complete stranger.

- **Reputation.** If all of your uncles and cousins are known as good-for-nothing ne'er-do-wells, news of "another one" moving to town may not be greeted warmly. This is particularly true in the South, where the stability of families and communities has allowed such generalizations to frequently hold water.

- **Differing judgments.** Your niece may love this ski town because she works at the resort and skis every day. If you don't ski, you need to take her comments with a grain of salt.

- **Differing lifestyles.** Will you clash with your relatives? Does your cousin work for a coal mine while you are an ardent environmentalist? Would your moving to town be a burden on your cousin, creating difficult career or social situations?

- **Availability.** Do your friends and relatives have the time and willingness to help you? Is your relationship close enough? You'll also want to be careful about becoming too dependent and abusing the relationship.

The trickiest balancing act comes when you're moving to a small town for romance. You've fallen in love with someone who lives there and you want to be close to him or her. On one hand, you need to establish your own personality. On the other hand, you want to devote as much time as possible to the relationship.

It's a constant battle. If you stick too close to your beloved, your dependence could strain the relationship. And yet when you try to meet people on your own, you'll still be labeled "so-and-so's new flame."

Simply being aware of the balance is an important step. As you cultivate your outside interests, other locals will grow to appreciate and respect your personality. As you communicate about your struggles and successes with your beloved, the relationship can continue to blossom.

Planned communities

In choosing where you want to live, you may want to consider a "private planned community." In such locations, a private developer creates an entire small town.

Planned communities are typically geared toward specific interests and may be near ski or (especially) golf resorts. They may be retirement villages, such as those frequently found in Arizona and Florida. They are often marketed toward a specific brand of potential resident. People who move to such places thus frequently cite being surrounded by a compatible group of like-minded people as a major benefit.

Because they're planned and brought about by a single developer, these neighborhoods offer advantages, such as:

- All new homes (or mixtures of homes, townhouses and condos).

- Efficient and thorough provision of municipal services, often on a wider scope than regular municipalities, by the neighborhood association.

- Organized social and recreational opportunities, such as activities and trips.

- A lack of "old-timers" (in a generational sense), leading to fewer problems of "insiderism."

- Strict (and upfront) rules about the types of behavior allowed. Such neighborhoods may restrict mobile homes, yards full of junk or parties running past midnight.

I must admit, such a neighborhood sounds to me like a nightmare. And it doesn't sound to me at all like a small town. I don't want rules on the number of pets or children I can have, how often I must mow my lawn or what color I can paint my house. What's the sense in having a great pool if I can't go skinny-dipping at midnight? I also believe well-functioning communities have visible ties to their history and natural surroundings. Most importantly, I don't want to be surrounded by "like-minded people." I want variety.

I also believe that a community should govern itself (difficult and time-consuming as that may be), rather than letting a corporation do it. A major lesson of failed federal housing projects is that too much centralized planning saps residents of their sense of community and thus, their happiness.

Some such communities are gated, with private security forces and private provision of other municipal services, such as road or sidewalk maintenance. (Some such communities even argue that their contributions to these private enterprises should exempt them from local taxes.) I find this attitude dangerously close to secession. The point of American democracy is that we're all in this together; we all need to work together to find solutions.

However, if a planned community appeals to you even after such a diatribe (and many such communities, particularly smaller ones, are not bad as what I'm painting here), investigate some. A good place to start would be the book by Lester Giese *et. al.*, listed in the Appendix.

20 Questions:
Choosing your destination

1. What are your geographic criteria? Questions 2-12 will help you hone them.

2. What kind of weather are you looking for? What weather can you not tolerate?

3. How close do you need to be to a hospital?

4. A shopping mall? What stores should it contain?

5. A grocery store, hardware store, auto mechanic?

6. A gourmet coffee shop? A McDonald's? Bagels? A deli? Gourmet pizza?

7. A library? A university?

8. Museums, theater or other arts opportunities?

9. A major-league sports franchise? Do you need four major sports or just one? And do you want to be near a *specific* team's home or just have the opportunity to go to a game?

10. A major airport?

11. Certain types of recreation? What are they?

12. Friends or relatives who live in _____ (insert city or town name here)?

13. Where have you been—or where might you be soon— offered a job?

14. Where does your spouse or partner want to move?

15. Where did you grow up? Have you ever dreamed of returning there?

16. What are some small towns you have always enjoyed, found interesting or wanted to learn more about?

17. What small towns do your friends and relatives recommend or think might be interesting?

18. What regions have you enjoyed as the settings for movies or books?

19. What small towns do ratings books recommend?

20. What places do your favorite specialty magazines, hobby or recreation associations recommend?

B. The components of small-town success

You want to choose a successful small town. But what do we mean when we refer to a community's "success"?

Many people think of growth. In a marketplace of communities, successful ones attract more customers and grow. So the current vogue of small town migration might suggest that small towns as a whole are successful market enterprises.

Actually that groundswell of migration isn't as big as you might think. Demographic data do not yet support the popular notion that everyone in the United States is moving from a city to a small town. True, non-metropolitan areas grew by 3.9 percent, or 2.1 million people, in the 1980s—but metropolitan areas grew by 11.6 percent, or 20 million people, according to Census Bureau data reported in G. Scott Thomas's book *Where to Make Money*. Other Census data, these compiled by Carl Haub of the Population Reference Bureau and reported in the *Christian Science Monitor*, are even more extreme. This interpretation suggests that non-metropolitan areas lost 100,000 people in the years

1990 to 1991—an improvement over losing 300,000 in 1985 to 1986, but hardly growth.

Think back to the 1970s, another time of perceived urban-rural migration, with newly coined words such as "penturbia" coming into vogue. It was a passing fad. Rural depopulation returned in the 80s. While the small-town trend seems to be returning in the 90s, perhaps it's just fad nostalgia, like our odd fascination with bad 70s pop music.

Growth *has* boomed in smaller cities (as opposed to small towns). Such places include new metropolises such as Orlando, Fla., or Charlotte, N.C.; "edge cities" such as those outside of Houston or Chicago; and smaller cities such as Boise, Idaho, or Albuquerque, N.M. If you judge small towns against the growth of these booming cities, most will fall far short.

The fact is, small towns differ. If you've talked about small towns with friends, their responses have likely been in one of two categories: They agree that it would be great to live in a simple, peaceful, friendly community...or they think you're crazy to move to the middle of nowhere where you'll be surrounded by nobodies. You may have chalked this difference up to their differing personalities. But there's another possible explanation: They're talking about different places.

You're probably familiar with criteria for describing cities as "good" or "bad." A city might be known for its great cultural opportunities, architecture, cuisine, educational institutions or park system. Or it may be reviled for its traffic, belligerent residents, racial problems, corruption or crime.

Why should small towns be different? There are both good small towns and bad ones. Granted, you can't judge the criteria on the same scale. A small town can have comparatively great architecture...for the full three blocks of its downtown. It can have comparatively good educational opportunities...regarding new techniques for growing potatoes. It can have corrupt officials...whose take is in three or four figures rather than five or six.

The good small towns are booming. The bad ones are dying. The dying towns are typically remote, insular, insipid and stifling. The ones that boom, on the other hand, possess a magical combination of quiet and sophistication, natural beauty and economic opportunity. Buoyed by the varying backgrounds and talents of the influx of newcomers, such towns have minimized (though not eliminated) the sense of suffocation that often comes with a small population.

Which types of small places are booming? Using strictly economic criteria, Philip Burgess of the Center for the New West, a Denver think tank, suggests they fall into four categories:

- Urban spillover, including newly minted edge cities and their formerly remote suburbs.

- Retirement, including places that are built for or have targeted older Americans, including early retirees.

- Recreation, including what Rand McNally calls "mild and wild" areas.

- Manufacturing, for those small towns lucky enough to retain or attract that Holy Grail of "good jobs at good wages."

But the magic of small town growth is not entirely "white magic." In fact, growth may be an entirely inappropriate criterion to judge small-town success. Growth is good for a city, because it can mean more interesting restaurants, more skyscrapers, more people to support arts and culture. The advantages of urban life are generally enhanced by growth. But the opposite is true for small towns. As a small town grows, eventually it is no longer small. Many people argue that an influx of urban refugees will simply spread urban blight. If a small town grows too much, too quickly, it can lose the neighborliness, community, tradition and inexpensive cost of living that made it desirable in the first place. (The Appendix lists some fascinating books on this conundrum.)

In general, as an urban refugee, you probably want your small town to possess at least these two qualities:

- Cosmopolitan.
- Friendly.

A cosmopolitan flavor does not necessarily depend on size. Take wealthy communities such as Aspen, Colo., or Hilton Head Island, S.C.; or artsy communities such as Taos, N.M., or Provincetown, Mass. These may feel far more cosmopolitan than "blue-collar" cities 10 times their size. They may even feel more cosmopolitan than a new metropolis whose culture has yet to catch up to its population. Regardless of how they stack up nationally, when you're selecting a small town, just one restaurant serving food you enjoy is a welcome improvement over none. A town with a part-time library may prove far more livable than one with no library at all. If you will have a small house and many visitors, just one decent nearby motel may be extremely valuable.

Successful small towns: Monique Sera

Monique Sera knew she wanted to leave Los Angeles. "I was tired of the fast pace," she says. "After living many years in the L.A. area and raising my children, I wanted to get away and find a place to relax." Evaluating her motivations helped her decide where she wanted to move. "I wanted a nice climate, open space, less traffic and access to nature. But I also wanted to be conveniently located close to a city."

Monique chose Desert Hot Springs, a resort community just 90 minutes from Los Angeles and 15 minutes from Palm Springs. "It's a spa town with natural mineral water, and I have enjoyed visiting here for many years," she says. "There are tourists from all over the United States and Europe." She found many of the benefits of a small town: "There's a lot of togetherness. I felt welcomed by people. I make friends easily. There is less driving distance for most errands and less traffic for driving longer distances." She also enjoys the casual atmosphere. "I can go out a lot more. Dancing, for example. Or just meeting friends for dinner on the spur of the moment."

Some aspects of her life are less convenient. "There's no good car wash in town," she says. "Choices of businesses are fewer. Though housing is less, costs for services are higher. Although I found most businesses offer excellent quality products and service, a few have a very poor attitude toward customers."

However, she finds those tradeoffs worthwhile. "I love the atmosphere. I love the silence and listening to the sound of the wind at night." She enjoys the closeness of the community. "Networking among local business people seems to be much easier here. You meet the same people at the spas and restaurants or even at the gas station."

She has taken advantage of this in starting a business for database management, computer consulting and mailing services. "The closeness of the community has helped me feel comfortable starting my business. Running my own business wasn't the reason to move here, but it's certainly become a reason to stay for a while."

People in cities (particularly in the Northeast) will overlook reserve or surliness in fellow citizens because there's so much to make up for it: challenging career, good friends, interesting activities. But when you move to a small town (often giving up that career or those activities), you're looking for that friendly, open feeling. That friendliness can vary. As noted previously, some small towns are extremely friendly—as long as you were born there. Some, especially those that have fallen on particularly hard times, may be known as mean places even among their natives. Many, however, welcome newcomers.

For me, the criteria for a successful small town also included economic diversity, a lack of fast food outlets or other national chain franchises, unique architecture, a strong historical character, a fun tavern, a cafe serving a worthwhile breakfast, a basketball court (and regular adult pickup game) and access to a daily newspaper with good comics and box scores. For you, obviously, the criteria differ. They may include ethnic diversity, the availability of higher education or proximity to your grandchildren. You may know these criteria intuitively, or you may have written them down in Chapter 1. Whichever way, you can use the following pages to help you judge towns against them.

As you do so, however, keep in mind the tradeoffs discussed at the end of Chapter 1. Make sure your criteria are realistic. High-paying jobs and low real-estate values? Unlikely. Low taxes and top-notch public schools? Hard to find. Proximity to an urban center and a lack of traffic congestion? Good luck. As Lisa Rogak writes in *Sticks*, "Don't set yourself up to be knocked for a loop. And don't try to bring the city's plusses with you or expect to find them out here."

So let's get specific. There are at least 15 factors you can use to evaluate a small town:

- Location.
- Institutions.
- Cost of living/economy.
- Jobs.
- Weather.
- Schools.
- Neighborhood.
- Safety.
- Entrepreneurial climate.
- Taxes.
- Medical services.
- Facilities for sports or other hobbies.
- Communications access.
- Landscape.
- Character of citizenry.

Again, remember that not every town will shine in every category. But not every category will be important to you. Use these evaluative criteria in combination with your own "gut feeling" to determine whether a certain community would work for you.

1. Location

The first three laws of real estate are:

1. Location.

2. Location.

3. Location.

The laws apply as easily to communities as they do to individual establishments. The location where you live will be of utmost importance in determining your happiness. It will dictate your job prospects, travel patterns and recreational habits. So choose carefully.

Your location will determine many of the other criteria we'll examine, including weather, landscape and the job market. A town may offer strong institutions, great schools and a low cost of living, but if you don't want to live in west Texas (or northern Michigan or southeast Georgia), you won't want to move there. Your location will determine the scenery and recreational amenities available to you, the town's history and, in many cases, its character.

It will also determine your travel patterns. For example, in moving to a small town, are you planning to frequently fly back to Cleveland to conduct business or see grandchildren? If so, you need easy access to an airport with good connections to Cleveland. Keep in mind that simply having an airport nearby may not be enough. Your airport may have one or two flights a day to a hub, which then has one or two flights to your destination. If you're conducting business, it may not be possible to do a one-day trip: You may not arrive until after lunch.

Also make sure you check on the convenience and stability of those connections. Do they use jets? Propeller-driven commuter planes are better than nothing, but far from the relaxed experience of a 727. Does more than one carrier serve your destination? (Are either or both of those airlines ones that you like or with which you have frequent flyer miles?) Ongoing deregulation of the transportation industry is reducing the cost of flying between hubs—at the expense of cost and convenience for remote destinations. Furthermore, flights to many remote areas are subsidized by the federal government—programs that may well be cut as our budgetary crises evolve.

Of course, flying is only one form of transportation. How close is your small town to an interstate highway? Such a road allows you to easily get to the nearby big city, the airport or anywhere in the country. A growing small town may experience traffic congestion on its two-lane roads (especially if they wind through mountain passes or country estates). Access to a freeway, on the other hand, will enable you to get out of town quickly.

You'll want to verify that roads are accessible and viable during all seasons. Your proximity to a city, or even a ski resort, may not be useful if the direct road there is closed all winter. And a long daily commute may be doubled by snow or mud in the winter and spring.

The Census Bureau collects data on the average length of a commute. If it's high, your small town may be acting mainly as a bedroom community for a nearby city. Consider the effects this might have:

- It can reduce the town's sense of community because people feel as much attachment to the city where they work as the town where they live.

- It can reduce the amount of free time people have to engage in recreational activities or serve in civic functions because they spend so much time on the road.

- It can spell trouble for the local economy as people do more and more shopping in the city on their way to and from work.

If moving to a small town involves lengthening your commute, ask yourself if this is really worthwhile. The pluses, of course, can include safer neighborhoods, perhaps a larger house and maybe better schools for your children. You may also be closer to recreational opportunities. On the other hand, long hours commuting may limit time you spend with your children. Which is more important to their development: each having their own bedroom...or each having significant quality time with their parents? Likewise, you may not have the energy to participate in your recreation of choice. You may find yourself spending 10 hours a week in the car so you can live at the lake, but then being too tired to use the lake except on weekends.

2. Institutions

Institutions create community. If you're moving to a small town, you're looking for community. So the stronger the town's institutions, the better the chances it has what you're looking for.

What do we mean by institutions? Everything from local government to annual town picnics. Churches, senior citizen centers, volunteer fire departments, chambers of commerce. Service and social clubs, such as Rotary, Junior League, Lions, American Legion or Elks. Historical societies, reading circles, arts organizations, planning and zoning commissions. Organized philanthropy. Day care. Long-term political groups (those that help define issues rather than presenting a brief flurry of response to them). Law enforcement. Libraries. Parent-teacher organizations. Parades. Festivals. Community events.

Most any activity in which residents regularly come together for a common purpose can be termed an institution. Such institutions create and foster a sense of community, both among people who work on them and people who benefit from them. Strong institutions indicate the residents' strong commitment to community life.

Strong institutions also play a role in improving the economic and political life of the town. Solid, trusted institutions can lead a community forward; weak or not-well-trusted institutions lead to divisions or stagnation. Philip Burgess of the Center for the New West cites a community's self-awareness, self-confidence and ability to plan for the future as key factors to success. He notes that these factors typically depend on the strength of local leadership and locally based civic groups.

All of this may be hard to accept, especially if you came of age in the 1960s. Institutions, especially the federal government, military and police, were the source of troubles. "The establishment" killed people in Vietnam and Kent State; denied rights to minorities and women; and frowned on sex, drugs and rock 'n' roll. Organized religion, federal bureaucracies and big business have been assailed for a variety of sins ever since. But our sense of community also has been assailed. For some people, particularly those embittered by past battles with institutions, a lack of community is acceptable (at least, more acceptable than the alternative). But those of you who want to move to a small town are searching for precisely the sense of community that strong institutions can provide.

Notice the objections to institutions: that they're mired in tradition, take away from our freedoms, restrict our individuality. Those objections stem from an urban point of view, one based on individualism and freedom rather than community. The small town has always been, and probably always will be, more trusting of institutions.

In moving to a small town, you need not change your mind that many institutions have promoted (and some continue to promote) inappropriate agendas. But you may need to change your mind that the idea of an institution is itself bad. *Local* institutions have done a great deal of productive and meaningful work at establishing and enhancing that sense of community you so desire. They thus deserve your support.

They also *need* your support. Local institutions in small towns are staffed by volunteers. These are people with careers and families, just like you. They simply realize that the sense of community they value takes work and commitment. You may be able to "freeload" off them for a while, but if all the newcomers to town are freeloaders, the institutions will eventually weaken—and so will the town.

How do you judge the strength of institutions? As we'll discuss later, a visit to the chamber of commerce can be very informative. You can learn from a variety of sources about festivals, celebrations and annual events. Ask around about the town's civic organizations. And simply keep your eyes open: A well-appointed historical or arts museum, paltry though it may be compared to your standards, may indicate a group with significant local support.

3. Cost of living

Chances are, if you're concerned about the cost of living, you're *very* concerned about it. While some people move with the vaguest of assurances that the cost of living is somehow lower than in the city, others want to do careful research on all aspects of the cost of living.

For those taking the informal approach, a glance at the newspaper is valuable. In the real estate section, you can get a sense for the average price of a three-bedroom home or the average rent for a one-bedroom apartment (if either of these commodities is not available, that tells you something, too—something bad). The entertainment section may list the price of a movie or the cover charge to hear a local band. The help wanted advertisements may list wages for typical area jobs. Grocery store advertisements will list the prices of their specials.

For those taking the more formal approach, a wealth of data is available, as long as you do some digging. Ratings books offer valuable statistics and comparisons, if you're considering a small town profiled in one of these books. The chamber of commerce may provide a "fact sheet" with information on major employers, demographics and quality-of-life statistics. If there's a local land-use or economic development plan that's both current and well-written (those are two big "ifs"), such a document might contain numerous economic and demographic statistics. A local library or university might be able to point you to other analyses. And finally, the original source for most of this data is the U.S. Census Bureau. If no local organization has analyzed and made use of these statistics (and by the way, that may say something about the local institutions), you can do so yourself by contacting the appropriate Census Bureau office.

Use statistics that are as specific as possible. Data aggregated to the state level is less useful than regional data, which is less useful than county data, which is less useful than data on the municipality itself.

As we've noted elsewhere, the cost of housing is a big factor in the cost of living, but not the only one. Be sure to also examine taxes (which are discussed below), utility bills, food, entertainment and incidentals. Most importantly, compare all of these to a realistic wage for the area—which may be far different from the one you're getting now.

4. Jobs

For most people, the availability of meaningful and well-paying jobs is a very important component of a town's success. A good job improves your quality of life by allowing you to be happy (or at least less depressed) when Monday morning rolls around. It can also improve the quality of your income, which can allow you to take advantage of recreational or travel opportunities or simply feed your family.

Of course, defining a good job (and thus where it can be found) is a very personal task. It's not something a book can do for you. (Though some books, such as *What Color is Your Parachute?*, can help you do it yourself. See the Appendix.) A software developer and a hard-rock miner will have very different ideas of good jobs and, consequently, of small towns that might possess them.

Furthermore, some people care more than others about the "quality" of their jobs. If you're retired or independently wealthy, it may make no difference at all to you how many good jobs are available in a town. In fact, as we'll see momentarily, you may prefer a place with fewer job opportunities. If you own a business with several employees and are looking to lower your labor costs, you may prefer a place with low wages. And if the great love of your life is surfing, rock-climbing or playing the saxophone, all you may want out of a job is that it put some coins in your pocket and give you plenty of time to pursue that sideline.

Conversely, many typical middle-class people have the problem of finding not just one job, but two—the town with the ideal job for you may offer zero possibilities for your spouse. The small economy is a distinct disadvantage in this regard.

As a rule, then, you'll probably find that **growth** creates increasing and improving job opportunities. As more people move into a town, there's a higher demand for all sorts of goods and services. And since many of these newcomers are from metropolitan areas, they may be demanding things with which you are familiar. Growing small towns often move (though very slowly) from simple agricultural economies to ones more resembling the contemporary urban scene. Thus you may be able to find a familiar niche more easily in a growing town.

Growing towns frequently present more opportunities:

- **There's more potential to move up or out**, rather than being stuck in a dead-end job. As the town expands, so may your place of business, creating new positions just as you're getting tired of your current responsibilities.

- **Growth means change**, which likely means that your job will be more challenging in a growing town. For example, a bank loan officer amidst a real-estate boom will be making far more interesting and risky loans than one in a stagnant backwater. Likewise, a journalist amidst that boom will have far more stories to report.

- **Growth often pushes and encourages an entrepreneurial climate** in the town. Growth creates a sunny optimism in the business community, and you may be able to borrow and harness this energy to help you realize your dreams of running your own show.

In the 1990s, growth trends have centered around two aspects of location, as we discussed earlier: scenery/recreational amenities and access to cities. Such areas include the Rocky Mountains, especially near Denver or Salt Lake City; the Sierra Nevada, notably in the area of Las Vegas, or Reno and Lake Tahoe; Florida and Arizona retirement meccas, particularly close to Orlando, Phoenix or Tuscon; and rural areas of the East Coast, such as New England or Pennsylvania.

As we discussed at the beginning of this section, however, as the area grows, it may lose its small-town feeling. Growth brings traffic, crime, ugly suburban development and stress—the very problems you were trying to escape. (This is why people not looking for a job may prefer a place with poor job prospects.) If you select a growing community because of its good job climate, you may find that the job continues successfully but the rest of the community doesn't. You may have to resign yourself to:

- Moving again in five years, when this place, too, becomes unbearable.

- Living with some degree of urban problems for the rest of your life.

- Working hard—and very likely in vain—at volunteer and political efforts to preserve that small-town feeling.

None of these options is particularly appealing. Then again, you may not much like the alternatives either: continuing to live in a metropolitan area, which may have problems but at least has plenty of job opportunities; or moving to a town that isn't growing (or is growing very slowly), which may not have *any* good jobs.

Keep in mind that the availability of jobs depends on your career. Certain skills, such as nursing, are in demand almost everywhere in the country. Technology allows more and more jobs to be performed anywhere in the country. Meanwhile, hands-on work in extractive industries—such as oil and gas development, mining or logging—is generally found in remote areas. If you want to work in agriculture or as a wilderness guide, your chances of finding a job obviously go up as the population density goes down.

5. Weather

It's the world's most popular conversation topic. It's the easiest to inquire about when you're learning about a new place. It's a constant source of complaint, wonder and enjoyment. It's the weather.

Many refugees of Northern climes, tired of being held hostage indoors for three to six months a year, flee to booming Sunbelt areas such as Arizona or Florida. Once there, they find the heat and/or humidity holds them hostage indoors for three to six months a year. Granted, it's a different three to six months, and the physical sensations of wandering outside are different, but when we look at the living patterns of people who live in the far North and far South—how much the weather affects their abilities to spend time outdoors—we see few differences.

We also see few differences in utility bills. As Richard Boyer and David Savageau note in *Places Rated Almanac*, air conditioning actually costs *more* than heating. You may well find your utility bills higher in the South than in the North.

So weather may not be as important as we might think. On the other hand, small town people *are* more apt to spend more time outdoors. Your motivations for moving may be tied to nature and/or outdoor recreation. You're looking forward to gardening, walking around the neighborhood with your dog and/or sitting on the front porch with a glass of iced tea. Consequently, weather may well be important to you, certainly more important than it is in the city.

Meanwhile, the physical setup of most small towns leaves you more exposed to the weather. There are fewer (if any) malls providing indoor shopping experiences. If you go shopping downtown, you will be going outside every time you go to a different store. And many small-town establishments—from shops to offices to restaurants—are less likely to have air conditioning because they don't have the capital to invest in it.

As we noted in Chapter 1, it's difficult to escape "dangerous" weather (such as earthquakes or floods). On the other hand, you can pick your danger. If you're tired of tornadoes, you could move to a place that has a volcano instead. Similarly, you can pick your weather extremity. Someone who has spent a lifetime clenched up against the cold may well enjoy the wilting heat of a Texas summer. Someone who's sick of San Francisco fog may well appreciate a North Dakota winter day when the sun shines brightly through windy, subzero temperatures.

In determining your weather criteria, include more than just temperature extremes. Also look at patterns: How often does it reach those extremes and how long does it stay there? How much precipitation are you comfortable with? How many sunny days do you want? Some places can be consistently overcast though they receive little rain. Check into humidity—it can make very hot or cold weather more uncomfortable. Wind can also exacerbate cold conditions—and make outdoor activities unpleasant. Finally, you may not want to be outside in even the most beautiful weather if the area is swarming with mosquitoes or other biting insects.

How can you find out about weather? Atlases and encyclopedias often provide regional information. Local chamber of commerce publications may list relevant data (accentuating the positive, of course). Most daily newspapers print some sort of nationwide weather map on which you can follow the daily highs and lows of your destination. And if you want to be really thorough, you can contact a regional office of the National Weather Service to get the source data.

6. Schools

If you have children (or are planning to), you're probably concerned about their education. One of your criteria for evaluating towns may be the quality of the school system and your kids' ability to get a meaningful start on life.

Unfortunately, it is true that many small-town school systems do not offer the same breadth of programming that larger school districts can afford. Many overemphasize sports, to the detriment of artistic and intellectual pursuits. Also, many rural school systems simply aren't as rigorous as they could be (or should be).

On the other hand, rural schools are far more likely to have low student-teacher ratios and they are far less likely than their urban counterparts to have problems of violence within the school building.

There are problem kids, drugs, crimes and teenage pregnancies, but school officials are generally more successful at keeping the school building as a place for learning.

Additionally, keep in mind that formal school learning is only one piece of your child's development. In the small town, your child may have greater access to learning opportunities outside of school by playing in the woods or starting a garden. However, rigorous intellectual or artistic pursuits may be more difficult to find. He or she may have a safer circle of friends, with fewer unwholesome temptations. And perhaps most importantly, moving to a small town could give your child a more productive, supportive home life. Kids learn by example. If your example is enjoying and appreciating your life, making smart choices and creating meaningful time for family activities, that may be the most valuable "education" you can provide.

If you are dissatisfied with public education, small towns generally have fewer private schools. What's more, the town's community focus may frown on private education.

Given that the quality of education can vary, here are some techniques to examine its effectiveness:

- **What is the school district's expenditure per pupil?**
  This is not necessarily a useful statistic, because a school district may simply be inefficient. But students in higher-spending districts may be more likely to have access to more sophisticated equipment (such as computer equipment). Additionally, higher expenditures may indicate higher levels of community support for the schools, which is always valuable.

  Note the difference between expenditures per pupil and per taxpayer. "Younger" school districts, with a larger percentage of schoolchildren, may have high costs per taxpayer but, nevertheless, smaller expenditures per pupil.

- **Talk to people in town**, especially as you get to know them. What do they think of the schools? How have their kids performed? What have their experiences been? Be sure to also ask them about their goals so that you're not comparing apples and oranges in terms of educational expectations.

- **Does the community regularly pass school bond issues?** In some states, schools must hold near-annual elections to determine the exact size of the bite they can take from your property taxes. Many towns almost always grant this privilege, but others regularly vote down the additional levies—which can result in larger class sizes and fewer "extra" activities (such as foreign languages). The no vote may be the result of a population that doesn't care about its children or of a poorly managed district that (in the voters' opinion) doesn't deserve the extra money. Either way, the result may be a poorer educational experience for your child.

- **Are there arts programs?** For example, is there an annual school play? You might check whether the arts teacher is full time, though you need to weigh the size of the school district into this calculation.

  Some small towns actually have excellent arts programs. For example, Kevin Mastellon put one of his daughters in public school, rather than the Catholic school he would have otherwise preferred, because of the quality of the music program in his town.

- **What colleges do the school's graduates attend?** Obviously many will go to nearby and/or state universities, but you might check if there's an Ivy Leaguer sprinkled in now and then (especially if you think your child might harbor such aspirations).

  A frequently cited statistic is the *percentage* of a school's graduates who attend college. I don't find this information necessarily helpful, especially in judging small-town schools. Plenty of people who don't go to college will nevertheless be productive, interesting people and valuable classmates for your child. If there is a large portion of non-college-bound students, peer pressure may work against further education, but these days that situation is extremely unusual.

- **What are the average SAT/ACT scores of college-bound students?** Due to regional differences, this statistic may be best used for comparisons among small towns, especially adjacent towns, rather than metropolitan areas.

• **Are there special education programs** (if your child requires one)? Are there gifted and talented programs?

• **Does the admissions department of your alma mater (or the colleges your child is interested in) have an opinion about this school system?** Admissions departments do judge high schools, though they may not be willing to share this information. Still, if you phrase the question delicately—especially if you're comparing two or three options—they might be able to reinforce your judgments.

By the way, many prestigious colleges *like* getting students from out-of-the-way places. They see it as enhancing the diversity of their student body to have someone from, say, Nebraska. (Of course, once you move, your child may love Nebraska as much as you do, and refuse to go anywhere farther away than Lincoln.)

• **What are the average teacher salaries?** This is another statistic open to misinterpretation. Many talented teachers need and want to be well-rewarded and will move from poorly paying school districts to better-paying ones. On the other hand, some great teachers work for next to nothing. (This is particularly true in remote areas, where taking a teaching job in the next town may mean a 40-mile commute.) Additionally, the cost of living will play a role. Though these teachers may be less well-compensated than those in the city, it may translate to higher disposable income or a better quality of life...just like you're looking for.

• **Check with the state Department of Education, teachers' association or other regional bodies** to see if they have judgments or impressions of certain school systems.

Be sure to include your children (of whatever age) in this move. Give them plenty of time to prepare. Let your enthusiasm for the new place show. Be positive and focus on the benefits of the move—not just for you, but for the kids. What is it that they (as opposed to you) like to do, and can they still do it in the new location? Children need familiarity to hang the "newness" of their lives on and may need reassurance on things you take for granted: that, for example, the new place has baseball, television reception or lilac trees. (You may want to keep such familiarity in mind as you choose your small town: Is it a place where Ricky can still watch plenty of 76ers games on TV?) Your current living quarters may be the only home they've ever known—leaving it may be a particularly traumatic experience. This may apply even if they're 35 years old.

Find projects that apply especially to your kids. Take some time with them to explore schools, day care centers or playgrounds. Learn what activities are available for kids, such as hunting or fishing lessons. Let the kids help plan what their new bedrooms might look like or what to do with a corner of the backyard.

7. Neighborhood

Some people who move from an urban neighborhood to a small town are struck by the fact that they can't go to the corner for a newspaper. On the other hand, some people who move from residential suburbs are often struck that they *can*. Both sets of people tend to ascribe this quality to the small town they've moved to, but in fact it has as much to do with their *source* as their *destination*.

Both "neighborhood" and "remote" experiences are available in both suburbs and small towns. If you live (like I do) in the very center of a small town, you may go for days without starting the car. Yet if you live (like many of my friends do) in a residential neighborhood in the middle of one of the country's largest Standard Metropolitan Statistical Areas (SMSAs—the Census Bureau's official name for a city and its suburbs), you drive every time you leave the house.

Regardless of the town you choose, you also need to choose your location within that town—the town-versus-country debate. In your dream of rural life, are you running a farm or just a garden? How close are your neighbors? How long does it take you to get to the post office or grocery store?

Living patterns in modern America have centered around the idea of the town, and for good reasons. Perhaps the most important reason is infrastructure: In town you can hook up to city water and sewer lines, you have easy access to telephone and utility hookups, and the local government will plow your streets and often pick up your trash. In town, you can walk, bike or make a short drive to do your shopping, visit your friends or take your kids to Little League. Finally, the town is an easy way to create community: When you can see your neighbors, you're more apt to meet, greet and form bonds with them.

In the country, by contrast, you may have to dig your own water well and septic system, hire out plowing and garbage service (or do it yourself) and, for particularly remote locations, even pay the phone or power companies to hook you up to their systems. You may have to drive five or 10 miles every time you need a gallon of milk or a different fixture for a plumbing project.

Still, some people are country people. What they want is to get away from people—all people. They may want to live on a farm, with domestic animals, or in a remote cabin, with the possibility of seeing wild animals. They may want an uninterrupted vista or the chance to take long, lonely walks from right out the back door.

Which type are you? If there's any hesitation, here are some additional issues you might want to think about:

- **As a tourist, what do you enjoy doing?** Do you drive around in the country, stopping for hikes or picnics? Or do you walk around town, shopping or admiring the architecture?

- **How do you define "air quality"?** In town, you may be subject to smoke or odors from a local factory. On the other hand, your country paradise may be (if not now, then someday) adjacent to a feedlot, oil well or gravel pit.

- **What are your thoughts on noise?** Some people find the utter stillness of the country unnerving. Others fail to realize that to make a living, farmers sometimes must run heavy equipment at unusual hours.

Moving to a growing community? Then make sure you look ahead. Growth can overwhelm such towns, and you may find that even three or four years down the road, you're faced with problems as aggravating as those you left the city to escape. For example, is there a chance your country home will become overrun by suburbanization? If you really want the "country" feel, the only way to assure it is to own enough property that nobody can build nearby. (Being surrounded by government land, such as a national forest, can also be somewhat safe—though activities such as mining and logging are permitted on national forests. Check the local Forest's Management Plan to see what might happen to lands adjacent to your house.)

If you're moving into a corner of somebody's farm, you may be expecting that it will remain farmland forever. That's a risky assumption. Particularly in growing areas, the economics of farming are extremely difficult, and the farming family next door may eventually have to sell to a developer. (They may be as unhappy about it as you.) You could be stuck with not only the prospect of new neighbors right on top of you, but also the noise of housing construction.

Of course it's expensive to buy your privacy. Permanent solitude is by no means cheap. But if land is the most important thing to you, then it's where you want to put your money—not in an extra bathroom or a trip to Hawaii.

If you do acquire a large piece of land with the intention of keeping it out of development, you might consider putting a *conservation easement* on it. A conservation easement is a legal document attached to the deed stating that the land will never be developed. In the short term, it will decrease your property taxes (because you will not be taxed on the land's development potential). In the long term, it will also ensure that your wishes for how the property is managed will continue long after you cease owning it. (Information on conservation easements is available in the Appendix.)

If you're moving to a growing place, you might also keep in mind these other concerns:

- Are you one of the first to build in a subdivision? If so, what will the neighborhood look like when filled?

- Has the town implemented any sort of growth management plan? Could this plan (or its absence) direct growth toward your currently secluded spot?

- What will traffic patterns look like with twice as many cars on the road?

8. Communication capabilities

Communication plays a gigantic role in our modern economy and lifestyle. You'll want to be sure that your small town has the appropriate communication infrastructure to provide you with everything you need.

As we mentioned earlier, those of you in business might want to check **overnight delivery** companies. Do they serve town? (If your business or clients use one service in particular, make sure that company's service is available so you won't be using "the competition.") Is it true next-day service, or second-day? How early in the morning do they deliver? How late in the afternoon can you drop something off?

If you have a **cellular phone**, how's the reception in town? Hilly or mountainous areas may have large pockets of poor reception. If this includes your house, or the valley through which you commute to work, you may have to prepare to be incommunicado for parts of the day. (Of course, many would see that as a benefit.) Some super-remote areas may not have cellular phone service at all.

Even **traditional telephone systems** may be woefully inadequate for your needs. For example, some remote systems still don't have touch-tone service. In some areas, you may not be able to sign up with your favorite long-distance carrier and the quality of the transmission lines in some areas may not be high enough for your particularly powerful modem or fax. These are exceptions, not rules, and they're becoming less frequent. They generally apply only to very remote areas, but the effects can be devastating. In *Country Bound*, Marilyn and Tom Ross provide just a hint of the nightmares of trying to operate a professional consulting business with a jerry-rigged phone system. You'll get enough jokes from people about your remote location; you don't need to add to the fire that telephone service hasn't reached there yet.

Along similar lines, you may want to check to see if there is a **local access number** for the Internet or for your online provider (such as CompuServe or America Online). Paying long-distance charges to check your e-mail can add to your overhead quite quickly.

Finally, consider the availability of **cable television**. It may be a source of news for your work or a source of entertainment and education for your family. Given the lack of other news and entertainment options (e.g., fewer good newspapers and theaters), television may play an important role in your new life. Many small towns don't receive broadcast television (or get only one or two fuzzy channels), so you'll need cable or a satellite dish. While the cost of a dish and its reception are improving, they are nevertheless two additional factors you'll need to consider.

9. Entrepreneurial climate

If you're starting a business (or considering doing so or working for someone who's doing so), you'll be concerned about the town's entrepreneurial climate.

Where do new businesses typically do best? The conventional wisdom may surprise you. As G. Scott Thomas explains in *Where to Make Money*, new businesses typically do best in places that already have a lot of new businesses. Why? These places are typically growth areas. They have a lot of available capital. Bankers and other service providers are more accustomed to dealing with entrepreneurs. Other start-up businesses can act as role models. And for companies in technical fields, places that already have a lot of new businesses—even ones competing with yours—may have more residents with the appropriate technical background to be your employees. Also, it's nice to have a peer group to swap tales with. In a town without many start-up businesses, the fellow next to you at the donut shop may not easily identify with your complaints about employee health insurance or product distribution.

Bad news: This description does not well match most small towns. The places with the best entrepreneurial climate are typically "edge cities" near major hubs or perhaps "micropolitan" areas ("micropolitan," a term coined by Thomas in his book *The Rating Guide to Life in America's Small Cities*, refers to small cities that are outside metropolitan areas but are still bigger than most small towns).

Most small towns have few new businesses. They are less likely to have suppliers of your raw materials, professionals with expertise you may need or business "incubators" to help you get started. If starting the business is the major reason you're moving, and you anticipate needing a lot of this sort of help, you may need to look at larger communities that offer more of these amenities.

On the other hand, there's more to a business climate than business services and camaraderie. Many small towns offer advantages such as:

- Inexpensive labor.

- Low tax burden.

- High work ethic.

- Friendliness and cooperative spirit.

- Quality of life.

The last factor is the most important. A small town offers itself as a place you want to live. You may be able to find talented employees who agree with you. And when your life is easy, happy and stress-free, you may find your business heading in that direction also.

Furthermore, of course, the very lack of small businesses may well mean that a small town will welcome yours. Especially if you are planning to employ a good number of local people at "decent" wages, the town may bend over backwards to help you. If your dream involves both starting this company and living in this town, and you have the skill and determination to pull it off, then conventional wisdom shouldn't hold you back.

If you're looking at a retail business, you have special concerns—you have to get the market to come to you. In *Where to Make Money*, Thomas finds that new retail businesses do best in areas that have:

- New customers coming through the door.

- Affluence.

- Growth.

Again, this does not well describe small towns. There are few new customers coming through the door—indeed, everyone in town may have done so during your Grand Opening (since there was nothing else going on that night and you were offering free hors d'oeuvres). Small towns are generally not affluent—in fact, average annual spending is 20 percent greater in the city than the country, according to *Country Bound*. Most small towns are not experiencing rapid growth—what may seem like a huge influx to a town of 3,000 would hardly be noticed in a city of 300,000.

Of course, your market may be wider than the small town: You want to hit tourists as well. The key here is to determine whether you can make it through the slow season. You've dreamed of opening a gift shop, and you've noticed streets are mobbed on the Fourth of July. But what's the town like in November? (For that matter, what's it like on July 6 or 7, once the crowds of the long weekend are gone?) Can you make enough money during the busy season (or busy week) to survive the slow times?

A good place to find information on the town's entrepreneurial climate is the chamber of commerce. The chamber members are your fellow business people, with whom you'll be able to trade stories and pointers. The chamber staff (assuming it exists) is your best resource regarding the town. If, on your first visit, the chamber people seem surly or incompetent, they will probably remain so after you've moved and are looking for help in setting up your business.

Most chambers, however, are cordial and encouraging. Since their purpose is to promote the town's businesses, you may need to keep in mind that the pictures they paint will be on the rosy side. But they are aware that, if they're successful in bringing you to town, they'll have to deal with you regularly. The small community usually keeps them on the fair side of the truth.

10. Safety

Because the perception of safety is an important motivation in your move to a small town, you'll want to be sure your chosen destination indeed matches that perception.

Some small towns are actually quite violent places, according to statistics. Per capita murder rates can be high. On the other hand, most murder victims nationwide are acquainted with their assailants, and this is probably particularly true in small towns. You're less likely to get caught in a crossfire between drug dealers. You're less likely to get killed for walking into the wrong neighborhood wearing the wrong brand of sneakers. The more you have this sense of control over the potential for violent acts against you, the safer you'll feel.

You can get census data on rates of violent crime. Often this information is also aggregated in ratings books, chamber of commerce materials or other sources. Be sure the data is up-to-date: An influx of newcomers can change the town's character quickly.

As discussed previously, the safety of your natural surroundings may be equally important. (To be flip about it, there's no difference between getting killed by a bolt of lightning or a gun—you're still dead.) I don't know of any source that rates and quantifies all these different risks. (Indeed, that may be impossible because people's perceptions differ so widely.) Scientists may have deemed a nuclear power plant "safe," but that still doesn't mean a majority of people would want to live next door to it.

The best approach may be to decide for yourself what "environmental" hazards you are not willing to deal with. Earthquakes? Power lines? Hurricanes? Hazardous waste dumps? You could end up with an extensive list, and you may have to pare it so as not to eliminate every potential location in the country.

11. Taxes

No matter how small a town you move to, you can't escape the Internal Revenue Service. Taxes are a fact of life throughout the country, something that comes as an unpleasant surprise to tax protesters who try to hide in the hinterlands.

Nevertheless, you may be able to find a small town with a comparatively low tax burden. In a sense, taxes are really just a contributor to the cost of living, as discussed above. But the idea of a government taking away your hard-earned money so rankles some people that it deserves its own category.

There's no question that many states differ in how they assign their tax burden. Some states have no sales tax; others have no (or a very low) income tax. But they generally have to make up the revenue somewhere. For example, states with no sales tax are likely to have much higher-than-average property and/or income taxes. In this sense, perhaps the best way to "beat the system" would be to live in a state with low property and income taxes but shop in a low-sales-tax state right across the border. Unfortunately, the savings you'd realize from such an arrangement would probably only be in the hundreds (or maybe low thousands, if you're a big spender) of dollars a year—hardly worth giving up other quality-of-life factors.

Another thing to keep in mind about taxes is the services you get in return. Some states are less efficient than others, but some states have higher taxes because they do an excellent job of road maintenance, environmental protection or assisting start-up businesses. Many states also use "sneaky" ways of collecting revenues—ones you may not think of when calculating a tax burden. How much is a hunting or fishing license? How much for a driver's license, and how long do you have to wait in line, since your time is as important as money?

Moving to Oxford, Miss., Mary Beasley was concerned at the high cost of car registration ("license tags," as she calls them, or "plates," as they're known in some other places). On the other hand, Mississippi has no toll roads. In New York State, which she was using for comparison, she paid a tiny tax every time she got on the thruway. She has concluded that despite the "high taxes" of car registration, her overall tax expenditures for her car are lower in Mississippi.

Local taxes also play a role. And again, you may need to weigh the tax burden against the services you get for those taxes. Snow plowing, garbage pickup, parks and libraries may all come out of your city or county budget. Their presence may make you more comfortable with a higher tax burden. Most importantly, high-quality schools frequently require higher taxes to support them. (Even if your immediate family won't be using the schools, you are hoping to become part of a well-functioning community—education is probably one of its collective priorities.)

On the other hand, certain situations can cause a higher tax burden even when all other things are equal. As Lee and Saralee Rosenberg point out in *50 Fabulous Places to Raise Your Family*, local revenues depend on both an industrial and a residential base. If a town has little industry, your taxes may be higher because residents have to foot the entire tax bill. (You may decide this is worthwhile so as not to be living next to a smokestack.) The problem may be particularly acute in areas experiencing rapid growth. There is high demand for new municipal services: paved roads, plowing and maintenance, water and sewer hookups, fire and ambulance protection and so forth. Yet until the new houses are completed, they can't contribute new tax revenues. So you and the other existing taxpayers may be stuck (at least temporarily) with the bill for the new people coming in.

12. Medical services

If you are approaching your "golden years" or your health has always been variable, access to quality medical services will be very important to you. In particular, you may want a nearby emergency room, a veteran's hospital or specialists in one or more particular fields.

The quality of rural health care has been an increasing concern in the past 20 years. Because hospitals are becoming more technology-based and more capital-intensive, small rural hospitals are having trouble keeping up. Many have closed; others depend on uncertain subsidies for their survival. Meanwhile, the focus on "glamorous" medicine has drawn many of the most talented doctors into specialties, rather than the general "family practice" of a rural doctor. And many rural doctors prefer to work in a community with a hospital, so they can perform basic but hospital-dependent services such as delivering babies. Some remote areas find themselves struck with a painful double-whammy: The hospital closes, and then they're unable to keep good doctors.

There is, however, some good news counterbalancing the decline. First, many small cities have become outstanding regional medical centers. You may be way out in the "boondocks," but if you're within two hours of a medical center such as Rochester, Minn.; Hanover, N.H.; or Iowa City, Iowa, you can be assured of top-notch specialists. In fact, the ideal small town might feature a basic emergency room—so you don't have to drive two hours with a broken leg—and easy access to a medical center.

The second positive trend is the recent increase in physician's assistants. Physician's assistants (PAs) are halfway between a nurse and a doctor. They can treat minor illnesses and prescribe medications. They work under the regular supervision of a doctor, but need not be located in the same place. Thus a small town can have a resident PA who takes care of flu epidemics and stitches up bloody knees, while still referring more serious cases to his or her supervisory physician in a nearby city. (This is economically viable because the PA does not need as big a salary nor as much equipment as a full doctor.)

The third positive trend in rural medicine is that many doctors—like many of you in a wide variety of occupations—are starting to appreciate the lifestyle benefits of working in a small town. Rather than dealing with the hassles and politics of a big-city hospital, they get job satisfaction out of being a valued part of their communities. In the next several years, the small towns that are able to retain doctors may be retaining ones of continually higher quality.

It's fairly easy to get information on medical availability. Does the town have a hospital? A resident physician or PA? Reasonable access to the various special services you may require? These are all yes-or-no questions. What can be difficult, however, is determining the quality of the yes.

As this book was going to press, a doctor in rural Wyoming was going to trial for murder. He was charged with murdering several of his elderly patients. The motive was not clear, unless it was some attempt to "play God" in deciding unilaterally when an individual's life was no longer meaningful. But what was most striking about the doctor's case was his history. For the last 15 years he'd bounced around small towns in the Great Plains and Rocky Mountains, just ahead of accusations of incompetence. Yet each new small town, desperate for a medical professional, welcomed him. In many cases they didn't even check references. All they wanted was a doctor, regardless of his talent or reputation. Only when one Kansas town stood up with the murder accusation did the entire story come out, leaving his previous employers wondering whether the "incompetence" was in fact something more evil.

The point is, doctors—and entire hospitals—can be incompetent (or worse). And since this is literally a life-or-death situation, the risks of assuming competence may be substantial.

There is no easy answer. Incompetent doctors also exist in urban areas. Yet the nature of the doctor-patient relationship means that we are far less likely to be "smart shoppers" in choosing a doctor than in other situations. Nowhere is that more important than a small town, where your other options may be severely limited.

13. Facilities

Does your destination have facilities for your favorite sports or hobbies? Even if you're planning to start "a completely new life," chances are you will want to engage in many of the same activities you have in the past. A town that's a good fit for you will have those opportunities.

"There hasn't been much change in our activities," says Mary Beasley of her move from Buffalo, N.Y., to Oxford, Miss. "We like bowling, we enjoy lakes, we go swimming." Likewise, in moving from greater Boston to New Hampshire, Tom Forman continues to work out and swim four days a week at a health club. For both of these people, the availability of these forms of recreation has been a key to their success.

Facilities for many popular sports exist throughout the country. If your preferred relaxation is golf, bowling or softball, you'll probably find an outlet at least somewhat close to your new home. Your task will be to evaluate the quality and convenience of those experiences. Quality can vary quite a bit: You may find the local golf course too easy or too lacking in the scenic backdrop you're used to.

Some sports require additional facilities or people to play against. For example, many small towns don't have a health club (and very few have a personal trainer). Weightlifters may be able to use the high school gym at certain hours (once you've established yourself in town, you'll learn who has a key), but you won't find a stair climber anywhere.

Finally, if you enjoy unusual or obscure sports, such as squash or racquetball, there simply may be no courts in existence. Likewise, if your kids play soccer or lacrosse, there may be no equipment, no teammates and no coaches.

The availability of sports facilities may not be enough to "veto" a small town. But it certainly could help shape your evaluation of towns that fit well with your activities.

14. Landscape

As we've said earlier, geography is an important component in the character of a place. It will also contribute to your satisfaction with the town. What sort of landscape are you looking for?

Dramatic landscapes are currently in vogue. Ocean sunsets, mountain peaks and colorful foliage provoke oohs and ahhs. Some environmentalists refer to pictures of such spectacular landscapes as "ecoporn" because, as with a centerfold, you gorge on its physical beauty alone. But any place will have an inner character that should be equally important to you.

A similar view comes from what might sound like the opposite perspective. "You can't eat scenery," say jaded residents (or former residents) of beautiful areas. A well-functioning community must have jobs, not just pretty views. It must have caring, intelligent people, strong institutions and all the other components we've been talking about in this chapter.

So the proper question probably is *not*, "Is the scenery 'beautiful'?" You can find beauty in prairies, swamps or deserts, as long as you are familiar enough with them to know where to look.

Instead, the proper question may be, "Does the scenery work for me?" Does the landscape speak to those you're comfortable with or those you remember fondly from childhood? Mary Beasley found the rolling hills of central Mississippi reminiscent of upstate New York. Bob Renner found the ocean he'd always enjoyed in Coos Bay, Ore. Tom Forman returned to southwest New Hampshire, his first home in this country and the place where he and his wife met and married.

15. Neighbors

We've been talking about physical and institutional properties of small towns, but perhaps a town's most important component is the makeup and character of its citizenry. We've saved this topic for last because, while it's incredibly important, it's also incredibly difficult to measure and understand. And of course there's overlap: The people of the town build the institutions, schools and business community. The people are drawn or held to this place by weather and landscapes. All of our factors for success contribute to each other. In this section, we'll examine some basic questions about the people themselves, using three categories: demographics, tolerance and sophistication.

Demographics. There are some statistical truths about the makeup of a town's residents. They are both easy for you to discover and hard for the residents to change. They include age, ethnicity and religion.

What percentage of the town's residents is in your age bracket? These people will be your contemporaries, your friends. You need at least some people your age with whom you share outlooks, perspectives and experiences. For example, if you're considering having children, you'll want and need a town with other child-bearing couples and young families. (Especially important: If you're a single parent, you may want a town with other single parents.) In addition to playmates for your children, these people can provide sounding boards for your experiences. Likewise, if you're an early retiree, are there other early retirees in town? If not, you may find that your "contemporaries" can't match your interests or energy level.

Does the town have people of your ethnic background? This is particularly true if you are a member of a minority group, especially one that has been traditionally discriminated against. The town may well be tolerant, as we'll discuss in the next section, but you may still be a pioneer. You may be a flashpoint for odd ideas; you may be a token ("Let's get the Black/Indian/Asian/Hispanic perspective on this issue—Susan?"). Again, you'll have nobody to share your frustrations with. If you're comfortable in this role (or adept at shedding it), by all means go for it—you will be doing the community (and perhaps yourself) a great service. But if that sounds hard and painful, you might want to look for a place that better suits you.

Does the town have homogeneous religious beliefs? Some religious groups have a judgmental approach toward those who do not share their beliefs. If you do not belong to their church, you may never be accepted (or worse, you may be shunned) in their town. Some towns (and some religions or denominations) are more tolerant than others, but even then the sheer weight of homogeneity may be too great of a force. For example, if you're a devout Episcopalian and everyone in town is Methodist, are you going to drive 30 miles each Sunday to services? Are you going to feel left out when your neighbors attend church social gatherings?

Tolerance. Given that a small town's size inhibits diversity, it is important that small towns be tolerant of alternative viewpoints.

How has the community dealt with issues of race or "alternative" lifestyles, including anything from long hair to vegetarianism to homosexuality to driving a Saab?

Many small-town residents, through a combination of ignorance and fear, have attitudes you may find distasteful. How prevalent are these attitudes? How much acceptance have these attitudes gained in "respectable" circles (town government or church)? In this regard, you may be pleasantly surprised. Small towns, after all, are themselves alternatives. Many small-town people have opted out of the traditional American culture in which you move wherever your job takes you and acquire the latest and greatest consumer products. These small-town residents may tolerate and even respect your methods of expressing yourself in nontraditional ways—as long as you can convince them that you respect them and their expressions as well.

While difficult to measure, tolerance is perhaps one of the most important qualities you can desire in a community. As we noted in the section on gossip, the fact that everyone knows your business may not matter much to you—as long as you don't feel they're judging you. Knowing that your neighbors will be tolerant gives you more freedom to investigate new concepts, ideas or lifestyles. It gives you freedom, in this sense, to pursue some of the diversity and individualism of urban life.

Tolerance for new ideas also allows the community to grow and change. Change comes gradually to the small town, a quality that provides much of its satisfying "rootedness." But as change comes, the town's residents must be willing to flow with it. That philosophy may seem at odds with the small town's traditions and links to the past that provide so much of its appeal. But keep in mind two factors. First, you as a newcomer represent at least some small element of change. If the town can't accept any change, it can't accept you either. Second, change is an irrevocable factor in modern society. The town that ignores or resists change is the one that gets left by the wayside or overrun by the frenzy.

Finally, the community should be tolerant of newcomers. That's not to say residents should run and welcome you with open arms. The community's stability depends on having few newcomers and having most of those stay. You haven't proven yet that you'll stay. Unless it's a community of Native Americans, everyone's a newcomer of some sort or other. Successful communities find a balance in tolerating and even welcoming the addition of some new blood.

A community's tolerance is not something you can physically measure, but it is something people will talk about, if not exactly in those words. Ask residents about the character of the town. They may give one or more of the following responses:

- **"This town really pulls together."** This shows civic spirit, which is good, but doesn't say much about tolerance. They might all pull together because anyone who would pull the other way has been drawn and quartered.

- **"Most of the people in this town are pretty good folks."** Who are the people who aren't? Why aren't they? Such a statement could be an innocuous generalization, or it could be an indication that the town is broken into camps that don't tolerate each other.

- **"This town is full of good Christian people."** Substitute any denomination or religion; this should send up warning flags. Religious intolerance is probably the most virulent and easiest to fall into.

- **"We have our disagreements, but we come together when it counts."** This is a tolerant community: They can disagree (about politics, economics, religion or "morality"), but they come together on the things that are collectively important to them.

Sophistication. Many small town residents are surprisingly sophisticated, as we've noted elsewhere. They may be well-educated, well-traveled and articulate. But you won't necessarily find them in every small town in the country. You'll want to be sure the town you're evaluating has its share of people you'll enjoy.

When people speak of a town as sophisticated, they generally mean that it has had some exposure to the outside world. "Sophisticated," then, is the opposite of "parochial." Residents have the talent, time and good fortune to take an interest in culture, travel, education or world affairs. This often gives them more "enlightened" views on racial and sexual equality, and makes them interesting conversation partners.

Tourist towns and university towns are "best bets" at having been exposed to the outside world. Tourist towns are filled with people from elsewhere, at least part of the year. Some of the town's establishments and individuals depend on "city folk" for their livelihoods—they keep up on fads and fashions and may spread them to others in town. Tourists often want a "different" experience...but "not too different." Thus tourist towns tend to lean in sophisticated directions.

Popular culture: Northern Exposure

The television show *Northern Exposure*, depicting life in a small Alaska town, was extremely popular in my town. Several of us who didn't own television sets would gather at a local tavern to watch it—the only show we watched each week. One friend of mine explained it well: "It's a bunch of eccentric people who let each other be eccentric," she said. "Just like here."

It would be hard to picture the characters in this show getting along in a city. What would a New York doctor, a woman pilot, an ex-con turned radio philosopher, a pompous retired astronaut, an aspiring screenwriter/shaman, an elderly shopkeeper and a cafe/tavern owner ever have in common? The answer, here, is a sense of place. The show portrays an ideal community: It crosses ethnic, age, income and occupational boundaries. It ties together people of different interests and beliefs. It represents a microcosm of society at large.

Furthermore, all of the characters seem to share equally in building this community. Recognizing that only his money can bring the town a doctor, Maurice does so—without waiting for a government to tax him. And while he occasionally tries to lord his money over the others, they are usually able to ignore and/or forgive his arrogance. Meanwhile, lost in the depth of his philosophical musings, Chris never seems to catch on that nobody knows what he's talking about—or at least he never seems to mind. And though the conventions of drama suggest that the urban transplant should be a reassuringly heroic figure with whom most of the audience can identify, Joel often behaves like a jerk.

Perhaps this last feature explains why the show is popular among rural audiences as well as urban ones. The traditional Hollywood notion is that the outsider can "save" a small town (think of the plot of most Westerns). Or less frequently, the small-town values "save" the outsider from cynicism. Yet in *Northern Exposure*, the two never fully engage. Joel never changes the small town, nor does it fully change him. Both are continually surprised and puzzled by the other's habits. This is a plot device, which provides the tension of the show. But it also demonstrates the difficulties of changing character traits. Unlike Joel, you're moving to a small town voluntarily—you should hope to have fewer difficulties than Joel. But since the move requires changing your character, you can't necessarily expect to.

Others' views on community success

Different people have different ideas about the elements of a successful small town. The popular genre of ratings books contains some interesting twists on how to judge a small town. Some of the criteria they use (that are not included in the text) are as follows:

In *50 Fabulous Places to Raise Your Family*, Lee and Saralee Rosenberg examine:

- Environmental awareness.
- Growth: Is the town growing and happy about it?
- Scenic beauty.
- Housing diversity: Some towns simply have no houses at the upper or lower end of the scale.
- Weather: Is it one miserable season? (If you shiver through the winter, you don't want to also swelter through the summer.)

In *The 100 Best Small Towns in America*, Norman Crampton also examines:

- The percentage of nonwhites, which gives ethnic diversity.
- The percentage of 25- to 34-year-olds, because young ambitious people are often the first to leave a dying town.
- The number of physicians per capita, as an indication of the quality of medical care.
- The percentage of people with a college education, as an indicator of employment opportunities (it may be a weak correlation).
- Status as a county seat, as county seats have more business and legal activity.
- Presence of a daily newspaper.
- Presence of a college or other institution of higher learning.

In *Country Bound*, Marilyn and Tom Ross suggest you examine:

- The length of the growing season.
- The presence of a senior citizens' center (and transportation to and from it).
- The number and quality of playgrounds.
- Whether most rental apartments and houses will take pets.

In *Places Rated Almanac*, David Savageau and Richard Boyer also examine:

- Contributors to stress. Interestingly, they define these as mortgage foreclosures, divorces, high school dropouts, personal bankruptcies, abortions and new welfare cases. Also interesting is that Nevada and Alaska—two rural states—are the most stressful, using this definition.

- Mildness of climate, with the ideal being 65 degrees year-round.

- Number of violent crimes and property crimes per capita.

University towns are filled with ideas. The quest for knowledge is paramount (except on certain weekends, when it's surpassed by the quest for beer). Faculty and staff are well-educated, sophisticated people.

Talk to some people in your candidate towns about cultural opportunities and gauge their responses. If people in one town mention the tractor pull and the Bible Study at church, while people in another town mention community theater and carpooling to the symphony, you may find the choice between towns getting easier.

C. Acquiring information

How do you acquire the information you need to make these evaluations? How do you learn enough about a town to feel confident about moving there? Your sources of information should include the following (some of these are discussed in further detail in the Appendix):

Chamber of commerce relocation packet. Most chambers of commerce have a standard packet they send to people interested in the area. Call the chamber and ask them to send you one (or better yet, stop by and pick one up).

If you are a retiree, mention that fact. Some chambers have special "retiree relocation" programs. The Bartlesville, Okla., retirement program, for example, offers a free night's stay in a motel and meal vouchers.

Some chambers also have special programs for small businesses. In fact, you might mention any special circumstances regarding your move. Though many small-town chambers aren't large enough to have these special programs, often the director is one of the most knowledgeable, "connected" people in town and may be able to offer you good advice.

The chamber packet may include items such as the following:

• Brochure on the area.

• List of recreational opportunities.

• Real estate guide.

• Sample copy of local newspaper.

• Copy of local phone book.

• Advertisements and/or coupons for local businesses.

• Church directory.

• "Profile" of the town, featuring economic and demographic information.

Yellow pages. If a copy of the local yellow pages is not included in your chamber packet, order one directly from the phone company. How many donut shops are there in town? How many health clubs? Where is the nearest chiropractor? You may want to make in-person confirmation to ensure that the quality of these facilities or services is up to your standards.

Local newspaper subscription. Reading several issues of the paper will help give you a flavor of the town. Reading just one issue may not be enough—subscribe for several months. As noted above, newspaper advertisements can tell you a lot about real estate, jobs and the availability and prices of goods and services.

It may help your analysis of the situation if you're familiar with small-town papers. If not, you may be struck at first with the comparatively poor quality of the journalism and the "quaintness" of the front-page news. Such characteristics apply to numerous small-town newspapers and don't necessarily say anything about the character of this particular town. And you may want to ignore the letters to the editor section: It's often filled with idiotic ramblings that may not represent opinions of the majority of townspeople.

Don't stop with the "newspaper of record." You may also learn a lot from regional magazines or local "alternative" papers. The "alternative" may be oriented toward the arts, a political viewpoint or religious zealotry. That would tell you something right there.

Land use and economic development plans. If you know anything about either issue, you might ask for a copy of the local land-use plan and/or economic development plan. The first thing you'll learn is whether these documents exist and, if so, how recently they've been updated. Assuming they're useful documents, they may give you a clue toward the politics and outlook of the town. What does it see as its assets? Is it encouraging development? Is it doing so wisely, stridently, desperately? Does that type of development concur with what you want for your hometown?

If you don't know anything about these issues, this information may prove too technical to be of value to you. It may be most useful if you're comparing small towns. Which town is the most organized and thoughtful in planning for the future? These documents can help answer that question.

To get copies, check with the chamber of commerce, library and city and county government offices.

Historical and cultural books and articles. You can get a flavor of the town by learning about its history and culture. Call the local librarian to learn if any books or magazine articles have featured the town. Novels with a local setting may also be of interest. You may then be able to purchase these items at a local bookstore or get them on interlibrary loan.

Regional guidebooks. Tourist-oriented guidebooks, such as those available to members of the American Automobile Association, may contain sections on recreational and cultural opportunities in town. They may also list some area restaurants (though many good ones are often excluded from these listings).

The most important thing you can do to evaluate a town is to go there. Visit! No matter how good the job sounds, what kind of deal you're getting on the condo or how much people rave about the weather, visit!

There's no substitute for actually being there. Brochures and listings can't tell the whole story. Eat at the cafe. Go to the grocery store and check out the prices, the selection, the vegetables' freshness. Attend a church service. Have a beer at the tavern. Poke around the library. Check the selection at the video store. See how much house $125,000 can buy.

Talk to people. Ask how they like living there...and why. Learn what they value about the community and what they dislike about it. Ask about current politics or controversies. Ask about your hobbies or interests, whether they be quilting, minor-league baseball or the climate for the business you want to open.

You can learn a lot by just observing people, too. Do they smile or even say hi as they pass you on the street? Do they greet each other? Do they seem friendly and relaxed—happy? What kinds of cars (or trucks) do they drive? What kinds of gardens do they have? How well do they maintain their houses?

The best value of visiting is just soaking it in. Don't analyze, don't research, just let the place speak to you. What's the atmosphere? Are you comfortable? Do you fit in? Can you picture yourself living here—and being happy? Does it feel like home?

In the end, as discussed earlier, I believe your decision should come down to intuition. Set aside your guidebooks, ratings books and other research tools. Ignore for a moment your reasoned analyses and lists of benefits and drawbacks. Put down the book you're reading right now. Wander around town and ask yourself, "Is this me?" If it is—when it is—you'll know. You'll know overwhelmingly. Your knowledge will be confident and powerful and sure. *It's right*, you'll say. *This is home.*

20 Questions:
The town rating guide

1. What are the job prospects? Can you find work?

2. What is the cost of living compared to your expected income?

3. How cosmopolitan is the town? What are its cultural highlights? How have residents been exposed to the outside world?

4. How strong are local institutions and civic organizations?

5. Does the landscape work for you?

6. Do you like the weather? Have you experienced the place's seasonal extremes?

7. Do people there accept newcomers? Accept change in general?

8. Do roads and airports provide acceptable travel infrastructure? In all seasons?

9. Is there tolerance for alternative lifestyles, new ideas, personal freedoms? Or do people seem narrow-minded and closed-off?

10. Does the town provide the medical services you need? Are these of worthwhile quality?

11. What is the town's demographic makeup? Are there people of your age, ethnicity, education and religion?

12. Will your kids get a worthwhile education? Will the overall experience be a positive influence on their development?

13. Can you still do your favorite activities? Are there parks and/or facilities—as well as fellow enthusiasts?

14. Can you live with the tax burden (given the services you'll get in return)?

15. Will the communication infrastructure meet your needs?

16. Does this destination provide the type of neighborhood you're looking for? Does that neighborhood have stability...or will it look completely different in five years?

17. Is your daily commute a reasonable length or will it take away from the quality of life you seek?

18. Does the town have good ethnic diversity? Are residents tolerant of minorities?

19. Is the town as safe as you want?

20. If you dream of starting a new company, does this town have the right business climate and resources?

Chapter 3

Your small-town job

How can I make money in the small town?

If you've read this far, you've realized one of the tradeoffs of small-town living is that great jobs are hard to find. Small-town jobs are likely to be less challenging and less financially rewarding than those in the city. Furthermore, as an "outsider," you may have trouble discovering job openings. As an unknown, you may have trouble landing even the jobs you know about.

If you're still reading, all of this hasn't discouraged you. You still want to find the best job you can in your small town. That job search is the subject of this chapter. We'll start with some recommendations—places to look for job openings. Then we'll gradually expand to examine several components of the small-town economy and how they may affect your career. We'll include comments geared specifically toward people working at home, those hoping to harness the information superhighway and those considering starting their own business.

If you don't plan on having a job, or already have one lined up, you may be able to skim or skip this chapter. On the other hand, you may find it valuable in case you have to reenter the job market. The information also will help you understand the struggles your contemporaries may be facing.

Before we get started, there's an important issue of *attitude* we need to address. Remember that the small town doesn't owe you a job. The responsibility for finding and keeping worthwhile and satisfying work resides with one person: you. If an otherwise-perfect town is not forthcoming with a good job, you have two choices (and badmouthing the community is not one of them):

1. You can decide that having a good job is important enough that you're willing to put up with the hassles of the city.

2. You can decide that living in this town is important enough that you'll work to create your own good job. Take a less-than-exciting job and make it exciting. Take a job for its paycheck and find your meaning and excitement in other realms, such as family, community or recreation. Open your own business—you might end up creating good jobs not just for yourself but also for some of your neighbors.

A. How to find a job

You want the security of having a good job lined up before you move. That means you'll have to find a job when you don't live in town. A remote job search is always difficult because many small town jobs—like many city jobs—are networked. You have to know people to even know about openings, much less fill them.

However, many small-town jobs are certainly available through traditional channels. These might be good places to start:

- **Subscribe to the town newspaper(s).** You might also subscribe to a Sunday paper in a nearby big city for a wider range of jobs in a wider area. (Some professional jobs are only advertised in larger papers.) Read the help-wanted advertisements and respond.

  Many ads require you apply in person. These are frequently positions that involve serving the public, such as a store clerk or waitress. The employer will be interested in how you present yourself. You can try mailing information for such openings (though if they say no phone calls, disobeying instructions probably won't get you far). In the end, however, you probably can't get such a job without making a personal visit.

- **Check the help wanted ads in specialized publications for your profession.** Investigate any jobs located in your target area, even if you don't exactly meet the qualifications.

   You might also go a step further in studying these publications: Are firms in your target area starting up or expanding? Have they been awarded new contracts? Have they just hired a new vice president for your area of expertise? Has a competitor just hired away an employee with your job description? By being proactive, you may be able to save them the cost (and save yourself the uncertainty) of a full-blown job search.

- **Ask about regularly posted job openings** if there is a large employer in town, such as a manufacturing plant or university. If you're lucky, these may be in technologically accessible form, such as a computerized bulletin board or a telephone message system. You might regularly access this system and eventually find a job opening tailor-made for you. Check with the personnel department to see if such a system exists and, if so, how it works.

- **Surf the Net.** Many remote job listings are available in a variety of electronic forms. Browsing tools on the World Wide Web (such as "Yahoo" or "WebCrawler") often have employment categories. Newsgroups such as biz.jobs.offered and misc.jobs.offered have listings and/or discussion. Finally, online services such as CompuServe also have job listings and opportunities to network. See the Appendix for details.

- **Check with the local chamber of commerce and/or economic development organization.** Do they know of any businesses in town that may need your skills? If you have an idea for a business you want to start, they may also help you identify your potential market and competitors.

   The most effective way to get this information is probably through a personal visit, perhaps during one of your trips to check out the town. But if you have to do it remotely, you might want to start by writing a letter of introduction, including a resume. Indicate in the letter that you'll call on a specified day to follow up. Then do it.

- **Research publications that specialize by location.** For example, Lisa Rogak's newsletter *Sticks* (see the Appendix) provides Help Wanted listings for many different types of jobs—all located in rural areas.

- **Contact a local employment agency, job service or headhunter.** If there's none in town, try a nearby big city. Since these organizations regularly deal with people looking for jobs, a formal letter of introduction may not be needed. Call them on the phone, tell them about your goals and ask how they would recommend you proceed.

- **Convince your current employer to transfer you if there is a branch in your desired area.** In some cases, you may gain some leverage by telling them you're moving there anyway—but be ready if they call your bluff.

- **Hit up your current friends and co-workers for suggestions.** Don't be embarrassed: This is networking, and it's the best and most important strategy for finding a new job. Do they know of anyone who's hiring in your target area? Do they know good companies there you should investigate? Do they have friends there who can help you understand the local employment situation?

   Who turned you on to this town? Maybe that person has some leads. (If it's friends or relatives who live in town, they should have an excellent pipeline.)

If you're single and footloose, you can simply move on to a larger town, a different region or back to your old home. Perhaps you'll have less money in your pocket, but you'll have rich, valuable (even if un-comfortable) experiences to show for it. When you have a family, it's not so easy. Money goes faster, the essentials cost more, the move it-self becomes expensive...and uprooting your kids (and even your spouse) can be a traumatic experience for everyone involved. If you haven't been in the job market in a while, you may be surprised at how stacked against you it can seem. There are lots of people looking for jobs these days, and many employers no longer feel obligated to even send out rejection letters. This is especially true if you're from out of town.

So you don't think a job is important...

Moving to a small town is a dream you've always had.

Worrying about little administrative details like what your job will be could spoil your determination and positive feeling. Surely there must be something available. Why can't you just go for it?

If you are the "Just do it" type, then don't let any naysayers get you down. Plenty of people—including myself—successfully moved without worrying about a job until after arriving at their destination.

If you're talented, hardworking and able to get along with people, you should be able to find work almost anywhere. And if you're the type for whom things always seem to fall into your lap—mainly because you've worked hard to position your lap in just the right place—then your "luck" will probably follow you to any setting.

There's only one reason to not jump off that cliff and the reason may matter a great deal to you or not at all. The reason: You might fail. You might discover after three or six or 30 months that money's just too tight or interesting things to do during long work hours are too rare. And then what will you do?

That brings up a key issue in the small-town job search: the importance of personal knowledge. Personal knowledge of community members is often the dominant frame of reference for small-town residents. They aren't necessarily prejudiced against you as an outsider, they're simply prejudiced *for* members of their community. (You can't really blame them. Loyalty to community is precisely one of the small-town qualities you're seeking.)

You may need to get to know people in town to get a job. You can try to accomplish this before you move using some of the following techniques:

- **Do professional networking in the area.** Is there a regional chapter of your professional society? Attend one of their meetings or conferences to learn more about local jobs. Sometimes you can also find generic "networking parties" where ambitious professionals trade tips and business cards. Any opportunity to get to know people may improve your chances of being considered when there is a job opening.

- **Visit and get to know the community's "power brokers."** These might include people who are "connected to the pulse of the town," such as leaders of the chamber of commerce, local government, a church or other institutions. They might also include powerful people in your field, such as the hospital administrator or bank president.

  What do you tell them? Just that you like their town and you're interested in job opportunities there. Don't pressure them and don't condescend to them—don't present yourself as the savior to all of their problems (they may not think they *have* any problems). Just indicate your interests and skills and ask how you might fit in. Remember that this is networking, not a job application: A referral to someone else may be a great success.

- **Complete on-site research if you're considering starting a business.** What niche is it that you want to fill? What will labor and materials cost? Don't just look up these figures in your local library or on your personal computer: Go to the town and confirm them in person. Talk to businesses that may be your partners (or even your competitors). Their insights may help you hone your idea—or may lead you to a better one.

Obviously, the best way to get to know people is to actually live in town. You may want to consider moving to the town and *then* conducting your job search. It's risky—you may not find a job and may dwindle your savings looking for one. But in some cases you may decide the risks are worth taking. Here are some approaches to finding a good job and minimizing the risk:

- **Do temporary work.** Though secretarial help is the classic example, many temporary agencies now use all sorts of skilled workers. It's a great way to make a wide variety of contacts. Many companies frequently offer full-time jobs to temporary workers who impress them. Note: Use an established agency rather than trying to do it on your own. Your lack of a local track record is as much or more of a problem in this endeavor as in any other.

- **Take a job that's not your ideal.** Maybe you're overqualified or would prefer a different industry or higher wage. But this job will get you to town and pay your expenses while you lay the groundwork for moving into something more desirable.

- **Substitute teach.** This is, in a sense, temporary work within the school system. In many small towns, substitute teachers are in high demand (though wages may not reflect that fact). If you are a teacher, this helps introduce your skills to the administrators who may soon be interviewing you for an opening. If you're not a teacher, substituting still gives you a great opportunity and environment in which to network.

- **Establish your lifestyle without worrying about your job.** This plan only succeeds if you have a healthy savings account and a great deal of confidence in your ability to find work. But for some people, where they live is much more important than what they do. If you are this type of person, you may be happier pounding nails in your small town than having the "best" possible job in a location in which you are unhappy.

Karen Connelly took the go-and-research approach when she moved out of Washington, D.C. First she took a summer concessions position in Yellowstone National Park, which gave her the opportunity to explore several nearby towns. Then, after selecting Jackson Hole, Wyo., she got a job as a waitress. "Many small towns hire based on people they know," she says. "They don't do national searches. So I waited on tables while I did interviews."

Connelly's experience highlights an important point: You need not fear a "hole" in your resume. In some high-powered careers, especially on the East Coast, a six-month stint of waitressing or temping might suggest that you're not "serious" about your career, and thus a less desirable employee. Such a philosophy is rare in the small town. In fact, the opposite may be true. By taking the less-than-desirable job, you're indicating your commitment *to this town*, which may impress small-town employers.

A local address

Some experts recommend using a local address to find a local job. For example, you might rent a P.O. box or use your great-aunt's address and have her forward letters to you in the city. If you can easily work out the logistics, such an effort may be worthwhile. It shows some level of commitment to the town (though not as much as actually moving there). It may also ease some of the potential employers' concerns about your "outsider" status.

But it's no panacea. If it's logistically difficult, you may not want to bother. After all, your resume or job history information will reveal your current whereabouts. You also run the risk that they'll see your use of a local address as deceitful. More importantly, their biases against outsiders may run deeper than addresses.

1. **Many employers fear transience.** In resort communities especially, people who move in from somewhere else are apt not to stay long. If the employer will be investing a lot in your training or institutional knowledge, he'll want you to stick around. So he may look for someone who has already been in town five years or more who can *prove* (not just say) that she's in for the long run.

2. **People fear a difference in culture and habit.** For example, your brash New York sales techniques may offend reticent dairy farmers. Or your urban Californian speech patterns may confuse and alienate conservative Midwestern engineers.

In sum, the drawbacks you present as an outsider are hardly superficial. You *can* counteract them, but the solutions need to be more than superficial as well. Displaying politeness, intelligence, honesty and hard work are good places to start.

B. The small town's small economy

The economy of most rural areas is smaller and simpler than that of many urban areas. This means that available jobs tend to be generalized rather than specialized. They also tend to focus on things that everyone—rather than certain specialists—need.

For example, if you're a lawyer, you may do a lot of wills, taxes and real estate transactions in addition to your specialty of trial law. If you're an electrician, you'll do everything from simple switch replacements to major rewires to new construction. If you're a computer specialist, be ready to tutor people on their spreadsheets and dig through their printer foul-ups rather than selling them a whole lot of glitzy equipment.

If you're looking for a job in a small town, there's considerable advantage to having a marketable skill. A carpenter, plumber or carpet-layer, for example, can usually find work at better wages than most. You may face a problem of establishing credibility, but you may also be able to quickly fill a valuable niche.

The road is a bit more difficult for some professionals who offer services that many city dwellers can't live without—a lot of small-town people survive fine without them. A massage therapist, brew-master, acupuncturist or personal trainer may be so foreign to small-town residents that they're not even aware such professions exist. The town may have so few copy machines or foreign cars that a repair person for these items couldn't stay afloat. Since neither people nor businesses in the small town usually have much money to spend, they may well decide to skimp on such "extras" as an architect ("let the builder decide"), a graphic designer for the brochure or advertisement ("let the printer do it") or an interior decorator ("I can handle it myself"). One friend of mine, a graphic designer, found when she moved to our small town that to interest anyone in her services, she had to drop her rates so low they barely covered her fixed costs. Without her clients from her old (urban) location, she'd go out of business.

Many small towns can support one professional in a certain field— but only one. If you have a degree in library science but the town already has a librarian, you may have a long wait for that person to retire. In larger cities, not only would there be other libraries, but also there would be a chance that current librarians would advance to management, opening up entry-level positions.

The same holds true for a wide variety of administrative positions (school principal, water treatment plant supervisor, grocery store manager) and retail shops (bakery, hardware store, florist). There simply may not be enough business to support two people. It may be that you can do a better job than the current practitioner and thus put him or her out of business. But with the small town's community loyalty, that may be more difficult (not impossible, but difficult) to do.

The job waiting for you

Do you have a job lined up? Is it a firm offer? Have they said, "Yes, we want you to work here, you will start on this date at this salary?" Or did someone say, "Look me up when you get to town, perhaps we can do something together?"

Small-town folk are both informal and nice—sometimes it's hard to tell the difference. They're informal in often not bothering with contractual arrangements; they're nice in not wanting to say, "Look, there's really nothing here for you." You may want to politely inquire: "The move is a big step for me, and I just want to be sure we have everything squared away."

Is it a full-time, permanent position? Businesses with seasonal demand often hire for the season only. When the season ends and you're looking for a new job, you'll be competing with all the other seasonal employees. Sometimes—particularly in businesses that rely on tourist traffic—the employer could start cutting your shifts in the middle of the season if the demand isn't reaching expectations.

What if the job falls through? What if it goes bust? Do you have a backup plan? For a while I worked for a software developer located in a small town. We would joke that as the only technical writer in the county, I had great job security. But then the company experienced financial difficulties. Unique talents notwithstanding, I was laid off. And I was brought face-to-face with the reason there were no technical writers in the county: There were no technical writing jobs.

Not all towns, nor all occupations, offer such a gloomy perspective. Some small towns are blessed with one or more consistent, high-paying industries. Many others—especially those that lack glamorous scenery or recreation—have such a shortage of young, productive labor that they'll welcome a talented (or even untalented but hardworking) newcomer.

C. Working for a small business

The spirit of entrepreneurship is strong in most small towns. If you harbor similar aspirations, you may be encouraged by this atmosphere. However, it may take some adjustment. (This is especially true if you're used to a large corporation taking care of you.) Working for an entrepreneur can sometimes be a trying experience.

Working for a small business in a small town, you may have to do without on-premises day care, lavish pension plans, corporate discounts on movies or travel or other benefits of working for a large employer. You may even have to do without "regular" benefits, such as health insurance and paid vacations. In a crunch, there are no other divisions or resources to help complete the extra work—you may put in a lot of overtime. In a small-town, small-business setting, these conditions are frequent. When a company has just three employees, there's no room for a personnel department. When a start-up business is short on capital, paying employee health insurance may be deemed an unaffordable "extra." And in a place where jobs of any sort are scarce, you may not have much leverage to demand changes.

Small businesses are also highly unstable. If the company has one bad quarter, you could lose your job. Or if the boss decides to move—perhaps to an urban location that's closer to supplies or distribution networks—you may be asked to follow.

Sometimes, you're able to forgive such conditions and risks because you can see your boss, the entrepreneur, suffering hardships as well. Many entrepreneurs put their hearts and souls into their businesses, and the spirit of pursuing a dream can be infectious.

At the same time, an entrepreneur's high personal commitment to the business can create problems. "I'm still looking for a professional environment," said one highly skilled friend of mine who worked for three different establishments in town before giving up and moving back to a metropolitan area. "Businesses here make their decisions based on emotions. Or ego. I don't get paid well enough to put up with that." Even people who admire the risks an entrepreneur takes, and sympathize with her insecurities, may find her impossible to work for.

D. Specialized skills and the information superhighway

An ever-increasing perception holds that technological breakthroughs will soon (if they haven't already) allow you to do any job from anywhere. To the degree that this is true, it bodes well for your move to the small town.

Unfortunately it's not completely true yet. A majority of jobs still require you to show up at an office or other job site every day. Others require regular—though not constant—attendance. It remains considerably easier to "telecommute" from your suburban home, where you can always drive the 45 minutes to the office if necessary, than from a remote farmstead, where you may be literally a day or two away from the emergency.

There simply is no substitute for personal, face-to-face contact. Almost all jobs will involve some, so you may need to do a lot of traveling to collect important information, meet people or just make the sale. Many jobs will continue to consist primarily of face-to-face contact. As Robert Reich notes in *The Work of Nations*, the "new economy" may actually include an increased number of in-person service jobs, such as sales or nursing.

Taking your specialized, high-tech skill to the small town may mean that you do a lot of physical commuting as well as cyber-commuting. It can mean a lot of hard work. It may also mean (as it has for me) that you make less money than you would doing similar work in the city. On the other hand, the job is providing more money than you would make at other jobs in the small town...and you're getting more overall satisfaction than the city could provide.

Meanwhile, if success eludes you even temporarily on the information superhighway, your other options are limited. As noted above, there may simply be too little demand for your specialized skills—at least in the format you're familiar with. The key is to be open and flexible. When television producer Robyn Kratzer moved to Park City, Utah, she found herself overqualified for any potential job. Even when she commuted to Salt Lake City to be the highest-paid producer in town, she earned half what she did in Houston. On the other hand, Kratzer has now started her own business, which she believes Houston would not have supported. While Texas is floundering, she says, "Here it's booming. They need expertise in communications here because it's an unsophisticated market."

E. Working at home

Many people, such as Kratzer, combine moving to a small town with working at home. Competent, specialized people in all sorts of fields are fascinated by the idea of a commute measured in inches rather than miles. Nevertheless, there are some issues to beware of.

First, let's distinguish between two types of jobs that let you work at home:

- As an entrepreneur, you run your own business, be it small manufacturing, consulting or serving as an independent contractor.

- As a telecommuter, you have a traditional job for a traditional corporation, but perform most of your work at home. While many telecommuting jobs involve technology, such as phones, modems or fax, others are simply self-contained jobs that can be performed anywhere, such as sewing or editing.

Depending on which type of job you're considering, you may view the following discussion with different perspectives.

The first problem with working at home is the **loneliness** inherent in that setting. At an office, you have co-workers to bounce ideas off of, chat with during slow periods or help you relieve stress. At an office, it's much easier to feel like you're part of a group effort to accomplish something worthwhile. At home, you can try calling people on the phone or even going out for a cup of coffee, but isolation of your immediate situation may prove more than you're comfortable with.

The loneliness extends beyond the regular workday. At home, you don't have ready-made lunch companions or co-workers to join you in a Friday night cocktail. This work/social network is important to some people's job satisfaction and even job performance, as you can accomplish a lot (especially in team building and other "fuzzy" objectives) in such informal settings. Furthermore, if you're moving to a town where you don't know anybody, not having co-workers (who can introduce you to their friends and relatives) can make it doubly hard to meet people.

The home environment can also be **distracting** in the form of a television, children, a floor that needs waxing or a neighbor who loves to chat. You need to have a lot of discipline or really love your job to sit at your desk when a lovely spring day is blooming outside your window and your boss isn't looking over your shoulder.

When you work at home, you can sometimes have trouble being **taken seriously**. A surprisingly pervasive attitude holds that work takes place in an office. If you're home, you're considered either unprofessional or not really working. The attitude can come not just from your customers (which is bad enough), but also from friends and family members, who distract you with questions, complaints and activities they wouldn't dream of bothering you with if you were in a "real" office. You can reinforce that attitude if you don't firmly remind these interlopers that you're working. Set rules to limit their interruptions.

If you are a telecommuter, your manager just may take you less seriously—if not in your current job, then as a potentially promotable employee. By working at home, you're often effectively taking yourself off of the corporate ladder. You may be sending the message that you are willing to do this job forever. (If that is indeed how you feel, then there's no problem.) Often the only way to advance is by managing people, which requires the personal touch more than most tasks. It's difficult to supervise employees from a remote location.

If you're an entrepreneur, working at home may limit your potential expansion. Where would you put another machine? Would an employee with the specialized skills you need be available in the small town? If you hired someone, would you have them come to your home?

Working at home may require a larger **capital investment** than a regular job. Your computer or other working tools may come from your budget instead of the company's, especially if you really want this arrangement and decide to "sweeten the pot" by offering to use your own equipment. This equipment may need to be frequently upgraded. When you need a bigger hard drive, will your employer buy it? Or will your wage rates (and savings) cover it?

In the face of this heavier investment, you also face greater economic **uncertainty**. How much work can you realistically expect? If it falls through, can you do another job without having to move back to the city or having to dump all your new equipment?

Regardless of the economic outcome (and regardless of whether you are an entrepreneur or telecommuter), the new setup can be **stressful**, especially if you're moving at the same time. You have the stress of the new job, the stress of the new home and the stress of arranging the two. You need to meet friends, find customers, get the work done, get the house arranged, straighten out your inventory, find a decent restaurant, make several sales trips, work out your finances...and yet you made this move to decrease stress. In the short term, at least, you're increasing it. The long-term payoffs may make that worthwhile, but you want to include in your decisions the short-term costs to your quality of life.

F. Commuter marriages

If you're moving for one spouse's job, the other spouse's adjustment is a difficult issue. As Robyn Kratzer notes, "The spouse that isn't the reason for the move wonders, "Where do I fit in?""

One solution, or temporary solution, to this problem is the commuter marriage. The spouse with the new job can move to the new town while the other spouse stays in the old location. One or both spouses may try to work out some telecommuting or flex-time arrangements so they can spend more time together.

Most people who move to a small town have the goal of solidifying their personal lives by increasing their ties to their community. It's important to realize that if you're considering a commuter marriage, that goal is difficult to achieve. As a commuter spouse, you:

- Spend a lot more time on the road.

- Spend a lot more time at home, devoting quality time to your spouse.

- Spend more time at your job and less time in the community because you have effectively prioritized: 1) job, 2) marriage and 3) everything else.

If both jobs and the marriage are important to you, then you may indeed be successful at them. But it will be extremely difficult to be successful at the jobs, the marriage and as a meaningful participant (and thus a satisfied resident) in the small-town community. Of course, if you decide you value your marriage or careers more than living in a small town, that's hardly a negative. You have found meaningful things in your life, things worth investing in. Many residents of small towns— in unfulfilling jobs and/or relationships—would envy you.

Commuter marriages place a particular reliance on good transportation. You need good, fast, dependable roads and a rarely snowed-in airport. It's one thing to not be able to get out on a business trip. It's entirely different to not be able to get to your family.

G. Careerism

"Careerism" is a word I use to describe our society's belief that meaningful work is the most important thing in life. While not universal, the belief is surprisingly widespread among social and economic classes, genders and religions. It accounts for our tolerance and even admiration for people we call workaholics. It accounts for our societal mobility, always willing to move for a job. And it accounts for the "lost" feeling that many of us have upon retirement.

Giving it up. Some people reject careerism as they move to a small town. They give up their "good" jobs for the prospect of tending bar or clerking in a gift shop. They believe the benefits of rural life—from recreation to lack of stress to the "hometown" feel—will make up for the lack of career opportunities.

If you are in this boat, be aware that you are going against much of our culture's definition of self-fulfillment and happiness. People will always hound you: "Why don't you move back to New York and get a real job?" If you are turning your back on such a career (as opposed to never having had one), the decision to compromise or give up that "careerism" ideal will demand some personal attention.

Furthermore, you're considering giving up both your career and your urban life. In the small town, other opportunities for intellectual stimulation may not exist. You may have wanted to be "free" of your job so you could go to museums all day long—in the small town, you'll have neither job nor museums. A friend of mine recently decided to go back to graduate school. "Backpacking gets boring," she said. "The recreation isn't enough. I need to do something with my head, and this town just can't provide it for me."

In the end, of course, this is a decision that only you can make. You may indeed be one of the people who gets enough out of the rest of life to not need a career. If so, being able to realize that and capitalize on it may be the key to your success.

Not giving it up. If, like most Americans, you prefer to keep yourself rooted in your career, you also need to be aware of some of the potential pitfalls of small-town life.

First, the commitment to community life that we discuss throughout the book takes time and energy. Since you don't want to take that time and energy away from your family, it'll probably mean you have less time and energy for your career. Additionally, if moving to the small town increases your travel time (by increasing your daily commute to a larger city or your time on the road to distant clients), that will be another increased demand.

However, these are sacrifices you've made willingly to improve your quality of life. To feel like a part of this community and support this community which supports you, you need to invest some time in it that you might have spent otherwise. A better life does not appear magically. You have to work at it. If that means sacrificing part of your career commitment, then do so if it contributes to your overall happiness. (If you're *not* willing to make that sacrifice, if you prefer committing everything to your work, then why move? You know what makes you happy, and you can get it in the city as easily—or more easily—than the country.)

A second problem is that your job in the small town may not provide enough challenge. As noted above, jobs tend toward the general rather than the specialized. There aren't a lot of management positions because there isn't a lot to manage. If you're a doctor who loves specialized surgery, you will be frustrated treating a succession of viruses and strained ligaments. If you're an accountant who thrives on big, sophisticated budgets, the tax returns of little old ladies may fail to keep your interest. If you're a construction supervisor who loves the challenge of a skyscraper, you will be frustrated doing beach bungalows and bank branches.

Additionally, being a big fish in a small pond may not be enough for you. Kevin Mastellon of Watertown, N.Y., says that a predecessor as general manager of the television station left to take a network job near New York City. Mastellon asked him why he would leave the town he loved. "In a community this size," the friend responded, "the general manager of the only TV station is a big shot. But I want to find out if I can be important in a major place. I want to see if I have it in me to succeed at this bigger challenge."

A third problem is that you may not find enough support for your career in the small town. On the general level, the community is filled with people who have rejected careerism or dampened it to accommodate life in the small town. You may find these folks distressingly laid-back, especially if you come from intense areas of the East Coast.

On the specific level, you may not find the community of people centered around your career. As Joel Garreau notes in *Edge City*, career groups tend to cluster geographically. Prominent examples include computer manufacturers in Silicon Valley, insurance companies in Hartford, Conn., and screenwriters in Los Angeles. Within cities, too, there is often a hospital district, a financial district and a high-tech district. In many cases these companies or individuals can locate anywhere, but they choose to locate where they can find a community of people who share their career goals and visions. This network helps people find new jobs, find meaning in their current jobs or come up with solutions to vexing common problems. By moving to a small town, you give up that community. You may be the only biologist, engineer or furniture maker within 100 miles. You can't describe a problem to a fellow practitioner over lunch—unless you talk on the phone or through your modem. (This is one of the major reasons that Garreau predicts edge cities, not small towns, will be the wave of the future.)

There are plenty of exceptions: small-town residents who work hard at their careers. Many find these careers rewarding. But again, as a rule it's easier to have a rewarding career in the city if you're considering money, opportunity and support. In all likelihood, you will give up some of these living in a small town.

One of the biggest factors is money. In fact, many small-town residents work two or three jobs. Their monetary motivations can take several forms:

- Some take an unrelated job for the income, picking up weekend work as a waitress, for example.

- Some move into related fields, again for the income. A very small town may not be big enough to support full-time real estate agents, insurance agents and investment counselors. But a smart and trusted individual might combine the three.

- Some combine a regular job with an agricultural interest. Most farm or ranch operations require at least one source of outside income.

For some, the combination of jobs is philosophical. The realty/insurance/investment office, for example, may arise out of the proprietor's desire to help the financial situation of his friends in the agricultural community. The line between work and relaxation blurs. When is he relaxing with friends and when is he selling them insurance? In the small town's small community, you are less likely to distinguish between your work sphere and your home sphere. Work, home and community are all combined.

Kevin Mastellon, the TV station manager, tells this story: "On Easter Sunday, I got a call at home from a guy wondering why golf wasn't on at 2 p.m., like the newspaper said it would be. I put him on hold, called the station on our other line and found out it was supposed to be on at 3 p.m. So I told him. 'Oh, okay,' he said. 'Happy Easter.' " Mastellon's in-laws, visiting from New York City, were appalled that anyone would call him at home for such information. He attributes it to the fact that in a smaller town, you personally know the general manager of the TV station. (He's also aware that as a former on-air personality, he has high public recognition.) I would add that in the small town, it's more difficult to define your home and professional lives as different spheres.

Some people hate this interrelation. A teacher, for example, may not want to run into the parents of her students as she's eating breakfast in the cafe on Saturday morning. A personnel manager may not want people complaining to her about their jobs as she's walking into the movie theater. A counselor may not want to see her current or former patients when she goes out dancing on Saturday night.

Other people, however, can tolerate it or even thrive on it. One of the problems of modern society is that work increasingly fails to create the social bonds people desire, according to Robert Bellah and his colleagues in *Habits of the Heart*. The authors note that people are always trying to answer the following question: How am I and my activities related in morally meaningful ways with those of other, different Americans? The authors believe that the specialization of metropolitan life makes this question increasingly hard to answer. If you sometimes have problems distinguishing between work and play in the small town job and community you love, you're able to answer that question every day.

Thus, keeping yourself rooted in your career could be an exciting opportunity to revitalize your life with purpose and meaning. On the other hand, it could be more than you bargained for. Ask yourself if this sort of work/play unification is part of your motivation for moving to a small town. If so, structure your life accordingly.

H. Your personal security blanket

Given the uncertainty of the small-town job market, you may need some savings to tide you over in case your job doesn't work out. The exact amount of savings will vary based on your personal situation: How much do you spend per month? What's the average time between jobs in your field? What's your spouse's salary, if any? What would be the cost of moving back to the city, if you had to? Check with your accountant for specific advice.

Additionally, given the uncertainty of how you'll take to the small town, you may not want to burn your bridges when you leave the city. Can you return to your old job? Your old friends? Try to approach the move as a dream you've always wanted to act on. Phrase it that way to your friends and business acquaintances. Then, if it doesn't work out, you can move back and say, "Well, I guess I was wrong. It sure makes me appreciate what I've got here." This attitude will take some of the pressure off your situation in the small town. It'll give you peace of mind to know you can "fail" (and yet still call it a victory). In fact, this peace of mind may help you avoid that fate.

20 Questions:
What's my line?

1. Are you ready to make less money?

2. Are you ready for a generalized—rather than specialized—job?

3. Are you ready for the hardships of working for a small or start-up business?

4. If you want to be an entrepreneur, do you have the capital, skills in many areas and the guts? (You need all three.)

5. If you want to "telecommute," are you ready to a) Do a lot of traveling as well? b) Work harder, perhaps for less money? c) Not be taken seriously by others because you work at home? d) Spend your entire day alone? e) Set aside the distractions of working at home?

6. Is the town's economy big enough and sophisticated enough?

7. Is there enough support for your career interests? For example, are there other practitioners?

8. The distinctions between your work life, home life and community life may blur. Does this appeal to you?

9. Can you relax and look for a job without pressure? When you take it slow, opportunities may present themselves.

10. Can you get a transfer with your current employer?

11. Is there a job that's not perfect but gets you to town?

12. Have you considered signing up with a temporary agency?

13. Have you checked the help wanted ads in local and specialized publications?

14. Is there a local employment agency?

15. Can you use the Internet to close the distance gap?

16. Have you networked as much as you could?

17. Have you introduced yourself and your dreams to the chamber of commerce? Other "power brokers"?

18. If you have a job offer, how concrete is it? Is it a permanent, full-time position? And what's your backup plan?

19. Will the new job(s) end up making your life *more* stressful, rather than less? Will it allow you to devote enough time to your family and your community?

20. How will all this affect your spouse and/or family?

Chapter 4

Starting your new life

How can I handle this big adjustment?

The hardest part of moving to a small town comes after you get there. That may not be apparent as you contemplate the decision, choose your destination, rally your family, quit your job, pack your belongings and leave your friends. Those tasks sound difficult enough. But after you move, you have to set up your new life: your new home, new job, new friends, new places to go, new things to do—and new perspectives from your small-town neighbors on a variety of issues.

A friend of mine made this move a few years ago. It was a tormenting decision. She was very close to her family; she'd had the same job for several years (though she didn't like it much); she loved museums; and since she didn't like driving and didn't own a car, she relied exclusively on public transportation. She weighed all these factors against her desire to break out of her rut and find a better life. She thought that better life might come in Montana.

Unfortunately, her entire thought process focused on "breaking out" rather than "breaking in." What kind of job did she want (and was she qualified for)? What kind of neighborhood did she want to live in? Would she buy a car? How was she going to meet friends? What activities would she be involved in? In short, what would her new life look like? She hadn't asked any of these questions. She hoped the move would solve them for her. Instead, she found herself in an unfamiliar town with few friends, no job, no social outlets and no transportation. Her loneliness and depression only made it more difficult to go out and pursue these opportunities. After three months, she moved back to the city. (In a happy ending, she found a more satisfying job at which she soon met her future husband.)

Hard work: Robyn Kratzer

"Had I known what I was going to go through," says Robyn Kratzer of Park City, Utah, about starting her new life, "I would have found a bed to crawl under. I'm enjoying it now. I've experienced the positives. But in the first six months, I would have packed up and moved back in an instant.

"We'd be driving down the highway, with these spectacular views of snow-capped peaks, with elk in the foreground, and I'd be thinking, 'My God, I must be crazy. Most people would give their right arm to live here. Here all I can do is be homesick for a cement-filled metropolis of four million people.'"

Robyn and her husband didn't realize what a transition the move would be. She notes that, though the long term may be positive, the short term has brought some very real, tough changes. "You don't realize how complacent you've become," she adds. "You get set in your ways. I cried every day the first month, and I thought I *liked* change. I've traveled to foreign countries and I'm outgoing, but this was hard. It was worse than a foreign country because it was my own country. I'd had no idea there were so many differences."

Robyn discovered she wasn't dealing just with just cultural differences, but also with differences in her personal living patterns. "You have to start over again with your support network. I was used to the phone ringing constantly. When we left Houston, there were 65 people I wanted to personally say good-bye to. I had them specialized by topic: If I had a problem with X, I could call so-and-so. Suddenly, people I used to call every day were a long-distance call or a two-day drive away. And here I had no one."

Robyn had a particular problem because she was moving for her husband's job. "The spouse that isn't the reason for the move wonders 'Where do I fit in?' I had to realize *I* had to start over. And eventually, I became excited about recreating my life. It's like I've closed the old book, and I'm starting to write the new book."

Focus attention—before, during and after the move—on what you want your new life to be. It takes a lot of work. It's not impossible, and in many ways it's enjoyable, but it doesn't take care of itself.

In this chapter, we'll look at some ways for you to succeed in this endeavor, from philosophies you may want to adopt to specific tricks you can try. The chapter is broken into two sections: meeting people and acquiring things. But first we'll examine some of the character traits of people who pull this type of move off.

Keys to success: Kevin Mastellon

"There have been people I know who haven't been able to deal with living here," says Kevin Mastellon of Watertown, N.Y. "What they don't do is think about reaching out. It's only one hour to Syracuse, a few hours to Toronto or Montreal. There's a fine music school in Potsdam—if you need a concert, you can always head up there. And though we don't have major league sports, we have college hockey and basketball nearby.

"You have to explore. When I lived in New York City, I only went to the Statue of Liberty once. The only time I've been to the Empire State Building is when I took my daughter. And the same applies to this area. It's rich in history—the War of 1812, development of the paper and timber industries. But you have to search it out.

"You have to enjoy the opportunities there. I think of the chicken barbecue we had recently at the firehouse. That was a lot of fun—like a college beer blast. There's local theater, kids' organizations, plenty to do. And you can become involved quickly. There was a guy, new in town, who asked me, 'How do I get involved?' I said, 'You just did.' I was able to find some causes that would appreciate his talent."

Kevin admits that his job gives him a unique position in the town's civic culture. "When I became general manager [at the television station], my life changed. I was in demand by every volunteer organization in town: the hospital, United Way, chamber of commerce. In truth, I overdid it at first. But you can become a big-shot pretty fast, and that makes life very interesting."

And he believes that involvement is very important for people trying to adjust to life in a smaller town. "You have to decide: I am going to become a member of this community. If you sit on the couch and moan, you will leave. You will be unhappy and you will leave."

What types of people are likely to succeed in setting up their new lives in a small town? In general, it's people who already fit the personality type of the place they're moving to. For example, when I informed friends of my decision to move, several responded, "I've always thought of you as a small-town person." The implication was, "I could never figure out why you were living in the city to start with."

The people I interviewed for this book generally appreciated outdoor activities and civic involvement. They rarely felt the need to attend wild parties or museum benefits. And most importantly, they had a strong desire to feel connected to their geographic community—to know, appreciate and spend time with their neighbors.

Sociologist Pat Jobes, who found that 80 percent of the migrants to Bozeman, Mont., moved away within five years, also studied the characteristics of those who stayed. He found (annotated with my comments) that these people tended to be:

- **Older.** People in their 20s will try a new lifestyle, tire of it and move on.

- **Married with children.** The more stable their lives are, the more this move represents an investment they will not take lightly.

- **People who had not moved much in the past.** Perhaps such people are more motivated to make this situation work, where the itinerant ones will move again at the first sign of disappointment or trouble.

- **Outdoor recreationists.** Access to hiking, hunting or skiing is of major importance to their happiness and can't be found in the city.

- **Lower income.** People accustomed to lower incomes may be more willing to accept the types of jobs available in small towns. They're also less likely to be tempted back to the city by a lucrative job offer.

That last characteristic is particularly telling. Jobes found that at some (very low) income levels, the migrants didn't have the financial flexibility to make another move. It's a common joke in my town, told by some without a trace of humor: If you spent all your money moving here, you'll never again earn enough to move away.

A. Meeting people

Meeting people: Tom Forman

"You need to plan how you're going to connect with people," says Tom Forman, who moved from greater Boston to Peterborough, N.H. "It's people, people, people all the time. You may want to nose around and get to know people before you undertake the move."

If he had it to do over again, Tom says, he would do a better job of getting out and meeting people. He holds this belief despite involvements that sound exhausting even to people half his age. For example:

He and his wife regularly attend a nearby church. "We've met many friendly people. Some are Wyeth-type New Englanders, with interesting faces."

He joined a fitness center, where he swims four times a week.

He's active in a local chapter of the Anthroposophical Society, a worldwide movement centered around spiritual renewal with associated activities in many fields, such as education, medicine, farming and the arts.

In a related effort, he has started translating some material from German.

Tom notes that these activities bring a variety of side benefits. For example, he finds the translation work stimulating and useful— helping others in their efforts. It also gives him an increased sense of community because he's found others interested in the subject.

He considers himself to have some fairly radical notions about everything from politics to religion. And he's very careful about sharing those opinions. Speaking about his behavior in the church community in particular, he notes, "So far 'the oddball' has not found it appropriate to show his true colors."

But then he pauses and admits that it was the same in the large suburban church he came from. The question, he decides, seems to be whether you should subordinate some of your individuality to "fit in" to *any* community—regardless of its size or location.

The key to successfully starting your new life is meeting other people. As Tom Forman says, "It's people, people, people all the time."

Whatever your reasons for moving, whatever your satisfaction with your physical surroundings, you won't feel a part of the new community until you start getting out and meeting people.

Humans crave social interaction. This is even true—or especially true—of those who move to "the boonies." When there are fewer humans around, your interaction with those who are around becomes even more important.

In a place like New York City, there are so many people constantly surrounding you that you need to establish your personality and distinguish yourself from this mass of humanity. Even subconsciously, you think, *I'm more successful/intelligent/artistic/stylish than any of these people.*

In a small town, by contrast, there is no mass of humanity. There are fewer people around you, and it's quite easy to see how they differ from you. So you need to do the reverse: Your goal in the small town is to connect with people. If you try to differentiate or distinguish yourself, you'll end up incredibly lonely. By accentuating your similarities with people you meet, you'll overcome the drawbacks of that smaller pool of potential encounters.

As we've discussed, most people who live in a small town value its sense of community. Your task, as a new resident who wants to meet people and start your new life constructively, is to enter that community. Note that this is a unique feature of the small town. If you move to a place (like many suburbs) where people are focused on their careers, you devote energy to your career. If you move to a place (like some urban neighborhoods) where people are focused on the arts, you go to museums, galleries, concerts and/or readings. Small-town residents value their sense of community and focus on the institutions, activities and traditions that build and preserve it. You can ease your transition into the community by paying attention to these concerns.

1. Institutions

One excellent way to find common ground with your neighbors is to support local institutions. The biggest problem that people typically have in moving to a new place is feeling like an outsider. The best way to overcome this problem is to become an insider. This may seem obvious, but it's surprising how many people fail to make that logical leap. The best way to become an insider is to be a "joiner." Join things. As nearly every person I interviewed for this book said, "You have to get involved."

Local institutions: Rod Kimball

"I'm a Kiwanian and have been for 20 years," says Rod Kimball of Bartlesville, Okla. "When we moved here, I joined the Kiwanis Club, and we joined a church. We've found our envelope of friends coming from these activities."

When they reached retirement age, Rod and his wife sold their accounting business in Bakersfield, Calif. "We didn't get as much for the business as we wanted," he says, "so we had to move somewhere that could support us—somewhere where the cost of living was low."

Rod's wife had gone to school with a person who now lives in Bartlesville, and the three of them discussed the town at a reunion. The Kimballs also looked at Fayetteville, Ark., but really never seriously considered anywhere else. "We came through three times," he says. "We called the chamber of commerce. We looked at the comparative prices of groceries and appliances. We looked at what the area had to offer—here, it's proximity to Tulsa, which is 40 miles away. So it's not like you're stuck somewhere isolated."

"We priced and took pictures of eight or 10 houses. Then on the plane on the way back, we chose the house we wanted." Actually, their first choice had already sold, and their second choice turned out to require a lot more work than they'd expected. "We'd expected to move right in, but needed to do a lot with carpeting and wallpapering. All of that on top of the work it took to move. My advice is to have someone move you rather than do it yourself. We had so much stuff. The loading, driving and unloading can be rough, especially on someone my age."

The community, Rod says, has been great. "Our only problems have been with the house. We spent so much time on the house the first eight months that we're just now getting into town activities."

When you volunteer your time, people appreciate you. They appreciate you as an individual, as someone who cares about their community and as a potential acquaintance or friend. This is much more true of your time than your money. If you volunteer your money, they'll be appreciative, but more of your money than of you as a person. So don't just give the Little League some money to pay for umpires— volunteer to *be* an umpire (coach, chauffeur, grounds crew or whatever they need). Don't just write a check to an environmental organization— go to its meetings and volunteer to help set up for public events. Not only will you help the organization (and thus the community), but also you'll get to meet other people who may share your interests.

Your town may have any number of organizations to get involved in. Which one you choose depends on your interests and their needs. Be on the lookout for the following types of organizations:

- Literary.
- Theatrical.
- Fraternal.
- Historical.
- Environmental.
- Educational.
- Artistic.
- Commercial.
- Social.

Which ones strike a chord with you? Which ones have goals that appeal to you? Find them and wade on in.

It's better to join an existing organization than to try to start one of your own. Remember that your purpose is to blend into the community, rather than to try to change it. If there is no institution that exactly matches your interests, then go with the imperfect match. Find something peripheral to those interests or develop some new interests. As the word "institution" suggests, institutions do not spring up overnight, especially when hatched by an "outsider." Until you get to know people in town, you will find it difficult to enlist them in a cause.

A few years ago, a woman with a passion for literature moved to our town and started a reading series. She set up readings by local writers and advertised them through a variety of media. Nobody came. The readings collapsed after less than a month, and a month after that the woman moved away, probably embittered about our lack of literary awareness and cultural sophistication. The funny thing was, we already had a reading series, as well as a separate Great Books circle. The existing efforts didn't precisely match her own ideals in their scheduling or character, but they were the local institutions. Hers was not. By eschewing the local institutions and trying to mold the town in her image, she succeeded only in annoying her neighbors and—more importantly—making herself miserable.

Need some specific pointers on institutions you might join? Consider some of the following:

- Join the chamber of commerce and/or attend its social events.

- Become a volunteer firefighter or emergency medical technician.

- Attend church regularly.

- Join the historical society.

- Volunteer as a coach, chaperone or extracurricular leader for local schools.

The list is limited only by your personal interests and the availability of local institutions that can use your services. I say "only" because your interests can be quite diverse (and you can be interested in something without having expertise in it), and there are typically dozens of worthy local institutions. You may need to dig around or pay close attention to find some of them, and some may not know what to do with your offer to volunteer. But don't be discouraged—many will welcome you. The other limit on your volunteer activities is the time you have available for them. But unless you're in a high-profile position, such as bank president or school principal, you probably won't find the demands on your time overwhelming...at least for the first six months.

Three very strong institutions in almost all small towns are the volunteer fire department, chamber of commerce and senior citizens' center. Several people I interviewed for this book mentioned the fire department as a place that not only held their community together, but also provided an easy point of entry for newcomers. For example, Charlie Mitchell said he got to know many people in his area of rural upstate New York when his wife, a Methodist minister, gave the invocation at the volunteer firemen's banquet.

Fire department: Charlie Mitchell

For Charlie Mitchell, many adjustments of living in the country seemed to involve the fire department. "Many of the residences are quite remote, located on hilly, unpaved roads. This means the fire department and ambulance service may not get to you in time, so you realize that you have to be self-reliant," he says. "You decide to learn CPR."

The fire department also introduced him to many of his fellow residents. His wife, a Methodist minister, gave the invocation at the volunteer firemen's banquet—the two of them attended this event, which they might not have otherwise. "We each had the typical urban prejudices about folks living in 'the sticks': that they're narrow-minded, inbred and so on. We were pleasantly surprised and somewhat shamed to find that we were wrong."

Charlie teaches American Studies at Elmira College in upstate New York and lives in a rural area between the small cities of Elmira and Corning. The remoteness takes some getting used to, he says. "With a septic tank, you can't just pour bleach down the drain. And in the country, you don't walk to the market or the video store. Instead you drive to a mini-mall. You can't decide at 4:30 that you want to cook something for dinner that you don't have on hand—it takes too long to get to the market."

He's amused by the way people give directions. "They don't use route numbers and stoplights. They use landmarks that often aren't even marked. Things recognized only by locals. 'Turn left where the old red schoolhouse used to be.' Now, the old red schoolhouse hasn't been around for 40 years, but people still use it as a landmark."

Their entertainment and shopping patterns have changed. "We do more 'small-town-type' things now. I bowl; Brooke has line-danced. We've come to appreciate the value of a VCR—you're not going to get movies like *Pulp Fiction* or *The Shawshank Redemption* in the theater for long. And we rely heavily on mail order for clothes, home decorations, coffees, briefcases...even dog toys."

Take note that the volunteer fire department (which in some towns is combined with an emergency medical service) is an excellent example of the way a small town functions. The community bands together to provide such services for itself. In an area with a larger population, these services can be—and have to be—provided professionally and paid for with tax dollars. In the small town, your contribution comes not in the form of tax moneys, but in volunteering your time. That time yields more than fire prevention—it helps you bond with the other members of the community.

The chamber of commerce serves the interests and needs of the town's businesses. In tourist towns, especially, this can give the chamber a large agenda: everything from overseeing festivals and events to determining the commercial district's zoning and architecture. The chamber is the venue for businesspeople to cooperate and, in the absence of more specialized organizations, is almost a "support group" for people to trade stories about their business struggles and successes. Because entrepreneurs (shopkeepers and people with "cottage industries") generally make up a larger percentage of the small town's population, the chamber can take on a much greater importance than it does in the city.

The senior citizens' center provides a wide variety of activities for a town's older residents. Often these "elder statespeople" know a great deal about the history and character of the area. The center also often provides an outlet for people who might otherwise be bored or lonely, perhaps slipping in physical or mental stamina or grieving the loss of a loved one.

Small-town institutions may smack of attitudes and philosophies you've never dreamed of participating in. Many urban sophisticates can't imagine, for example, being part of a fraternal or service club such as the Eagles, Elks, Lions or Rotary. Others may want to decry the role of a grange, Rod and Gun Club or Ducks Unlimited chapter. Still others may fear or despise organized religion. But when you get to the small town, don't judge these organizations based on knee-jerk prejudices. Judge them on the quality of work they do in the community and the quality of the people involved in them.

Institutional activities make up of the fabric of small-town social life. You may have always thought that the only people who did these sorts of things were rural rubes with nothing better to do. But remember: In fulfilling your dream of moving to a small town, you've (proudly) become a rural rube yourself!

Personal relationships: Diane Heady-Reuss

"In the small town, personal relationships are much more important in conducting business," says Diane Heady-Reuss of Stockbridge, Massachusetts. "Make sure you get to know people at the local car dealers, banks, grocery stores and specialty markets, as well as public officials. Then when you need something, you can walk in and they're more likely to give it to you—once you've established that relationship. And establishing those relationships is easier to do here, because there are fewer people to get to know."

Diane moved from suburban Chicago to Stockbridge 11 years ago. "I'd known Stockbridge from visits in previous years," she says, "and I believed it to be a small, wonderful, happy place to live." Her husband retired, and the two of them got an art gallery, framing and selling art. Several years later, they started a bed-and-breakfast, the Roeder House, in their home.

Diane notes a big difference in dress. "Here, people dress much more crunchy-earthy than they do in the suburbs. People dress down: jeans, and heavy boots in the winter. People just aren't into clothes. It's a different emphasis—you spend money on winter clothes."

She also found a difference in the small community. "It's like living in a fishbowl, yes," she says. "But that becomes somehow irrelevant. The benefits far outweigh the minuses. If you forget your wallet, you can pay for something later. Or you can run an account, pay a monthly bill. You get great service, at the gas station or the car wash, for example. And you can live with your doors unlocked, and cars left open."

To support that ambiance, she shops locally as much as possible. "I do go to Albany, New York or Boston for major purchases, or when I'm looking for pizzazz or style. But money you spend in the local area turns over seven times. I want to support the county where I live. Doing so benefits everybody, including myself."

2. Activities

Here's a philosophy: Anything you do, consider doing it with others. In hoping to meet and make connections with other members of your community, you may want to focus on joint activities. In a big city, your home is your refuge from the onslaught of everyday life. In a small town, the community is the refuge. Rather than hiding from your fellow human beings, include them in your rituals and special events.

Do you head for the bakery every Monday at 11 a.m. for a cinnamon roll? Then sit at a table with some other "regulars." Going for a hike or a mountain bike ride? Invite an acquaintance. Taking the family on a picnic at the beach? Maybe the neighbors would want to join you.

Get involved: Roda Grubb

"My number one piece of advice is to get involved," says Roda Grubb of Crockett, Texas. "Get a list of civic clubs. Join a church. Join the chamber of commerce—many have individual members. It helps so much when you know somebody. They can help you pick a doctor. You may even meet one."

Roda moved to Crockett from the Dallas area in 1992 for her husband's job. She admits getting used to the new life was a struggle at first. "It can be hard. It depends on your personality and how willing you are to make the change." One of her biggest difficulties was finding the products and services she was used to. "We do have a hospital, and I think that's very important—to move someplace with a hospital. But we don't have a lot of natural foods, herbs or books. There's no foot doctor, no gynecologist. I had to find some other towns with these services. Wean myself. Sometimes I go stir-crazy: If I don't see a city, I go nuts."

But she has found advantages, too. "I'm more relaxed in dress. I don't wear heels every day—maybe once a week. I even wear flats to church. I'm more relaxed in my attitude about a lot of things. I don't feel I have to make an impression. People like me for me. I've gained self-confidence that way."

Roda says she's busier now than she was in Dallas. "We work an awful lot, and we spend leisure time in our house, yard and garden. We have 10 acres here, where we used to have just a half-acre."

She notes that getting involved is particularly important in very small towns, where everyone already knows each other. "Small towns can be very clique-ish. One man told me that at 5 p.m. everyone goes home, and they won't invite you to their homes. You could die of loneliness. I think only a church or a civic organization can get you through that."

Consider group activities or pastimes. Rather than sitting at home, try golfing or bowling. See if there's a community volleyball game. Spread the word that you're interested in joining a softball team. Accept an invitation to a poker game...at least a low-stakes poker game.

Expand your horizons. Do something you haven't done in a long time, if ever. Maybe it's attending a high-school sporting event or going to hunter education classes. In my first year in the small town, I attended an art opening, went to an iguana race, played in a marathon "Risk" (the board game) tournament and joined a meditation group. I had never done any of these activities before—nor even seriously considered them. Yet in each case I returned, though more because I liked the people than for any love of the activity itself.

3. Traditions

Four traditions enhance and support the small-town sense of community and your quality of life: neighborliness, property rights, good conversation and connecting with like-minded people.

Neighborliness. One of the benefits of small-town life, as Raye Ringholz writes in *Little Town Blues*, is "a diverse population that takes the time to be neighbors." That phrase nicely captures the components of small-town neighborliness: time and diversity.

Neighborliness takes time. It doesn't appear out of nowhere, unbidden. It doesn't reside in trees or Victorian houses or pretty scenery. It comes as the result of many people taking the time and effort to be courteous (and indeed, to go beyond that) to each other. In a panic to get to the bank before it closes? You won't have the time to say "hi" to people on the street. Scheming a marketing strategy as you wait in line at the post office? You won't have time to chat. Planning to do a whole season's worth of chores in one Saturday morning? You won't notice the guy next door leaning in invitation over the fence. The tradition of neighborliness is the tradition of a slower pace, a less ambitious lifestyle. You can't get one without the other.

Good neighbors are diverse, not homogenous. Neighborliness is not something you apply only to people you like. It holds for everyone in town. You act friendly, even if this person makes your blood boil. Does that sound like hypocrisy? Maybe it is. On the other hand, if you keep up the appearance of being friendly, sometimes you can forget what it was you were angry about. Regardless, this veneer helps define the community character. When you say of a place, "It's a friendly town," that doesn't necessarily mean everyone there gets along swimmingly. It may mean they've learned to disagree in a neighborly fashion.

Here's another tip that may sound obvious until you see how many people don't do it: Provide for your neighbors and fellow townspeople the same attitudes and services you expect from them. Do you like the fact that people say hi to strangers on the street? Then do so yourself. Would you like to find someone who would feed your cat or water your plants when you're out of town? Then volunteer to do it for them first. Do you long for the type of community where neighbors shovel the sidewalks or mow the lawns of people too elderly or handicapped to do it themselves? Then *be* that good neighbor. Create that sense of community yourself.

Property rights. There are two types of property in rural America: community property and private property. Community property is land used by almost everyone, such as a swimming hole, hiking trail or *de facto* dump. Private property belongs wholly and exclusively to the landowner, who often feels perfectly justified in shooting trespassers on sight.

The problem comes in telling the difference between the two types of property. It often has nothing to do with ownership. Some government land has "always" been leased to the same farm. Some private land has "always" been used for public purposes. How do you distinguish? The rules aren't written anywhere. You can't figure them out based on the landscape, zoning regulations or deed restrictions. They're based on tradition.

Did the previous owners of your land allow people to hunt on it or to cut through to a snowmobile path on the public land behind you? Then you may want to continue to allow these activities, regardless of your personal feelings about hunting or snowmobiling. This could gain you goodwill and some friends. You may want to discover this sort of information before you buy the land. If excluding community use is important to you, consider buying a different parcel. Of course, you may well have legal justification for halting public "rights" to your land. But if it goes against community tradition, it's sure to upset your new neighbors.

As a recreationist, you'll want to beware of private property. Does a pond on that farm look like a good bird-watching site? Then go up to the farmhouse and ask if you can use it next Tuesday. Tempted to use a wide spot in the irrigation ditch to cool off the kids on a summer day? Then find out who owns it and ask if you can swim there. Planning a three-day rafting trip through private lands? Then write or phone the owners and ask permission to set up your riverside camping spots.

This may sound unfair, even ridiculous. Property should be public or private, and it should be easy to tell the difference. People should cut you some slack as a newcomer: The onus shouldn't be on you to guess (and often guess wrong) or expend so much energy learning. Nevertheless, this is the way it is. These traditions have evolved over years, even centuries. They work—at least, they work well enough to create and support this community you want to be a part of. You owe it to the community to understand and uphold these traditions.

Conversation. As a newcomer in town, you'll find some subjects excellent fodder for conversation and others mined with potential difficulties. For example, don't start off your new life by telling people what to do with their property. The junked cars on the empty lot next door may infuriate you, but you knew they were there when you moved in. You may get a few allies for a "beautification" campaign, but the owners of that land will be sure enemies.

Likewise, don't tell people what to do with their political beliefs. For example, you may have strong feelings about gun control; you may even oppose hunting or be an animal-rights activist. But now is not the time to proselytize these views. Learn a bit first about your neighbors: why they value guns, why they appreciate hunting. Good hunters use the experience to connect with nature, not abuse it—in fact, they may be better environmentalists than you are. And many rural folk, with incomes so much smaller than yours, depend on the meat they get during hunting season to put food on the table.

You *can* talk about politics, but start in "asking" and "listening" mode, rather than "telling" mode. Become informed enough about local politics or issues to ask about them. For example, "What's the story with this development by the river?" or "What's the history behind this sales-tax initiative?" People shouldn't object to your ignorance as much as they would superiority or apathy.

Finally, don't tell people what to do with their community. Don't expect to breeze in and take over the City Council or Library Board. Don't expect that your educational background and business success will have people clamoring to send you to Washington.

Find ways you can resonate with others in the community. What do the natives respond to? What issues and values are important to them? Chances are you hold somewhat similar views. Discovering how you fit in can be an entertaining and rewarding experience for you. Your neighbors will also be flattered that you care about their beliefs.

As you talk about the local culture and its differences from the place you came from, remember that people are expecting you to appreciate their lifestyle. Never—ever—introduce a concept with, "This is how we did it back in California." That statement implies that California was better. People (especially the people who are invested in whatever you want to change) will say, "Why don't you just move back there, if it was so great?" Or "You moved here because California's been ruined, but now you want to turn this place into another California." *These are completely valid complaints.* If you learn only one thing from this book, I hope it is to develop attitudes that prevent others from making such comments.

If you must talk about your pet ideas, talk about them in the abstract. For example, let's say you want to start a recycling program. Instead of saying, "In California, it was great. We had curbside recycling," say, "How do you feel about curbside recycling? It seems important to me." *If* you start getting some support for the idea, then others may turn to you to ask how the California program worked. Always be careful to present California as a resource to learn from rather than a model to blindly emulate.

Of course, you can't suppress your personality, your moral beliefs and character. You want to deal honestly with your neighbors, painting a true portrait of yourself. On the other hand, in any social interaction, there's a balance between honesty and respect for others. Keep in mind that in the small town, we lean more—perhaps too much, for some people—to the latter. We do it because it supports the tradition of neighborliness and the tight-knit community.

Like-minded people. The above discussion may be frightening you into the notion that you won't find "our kind of people" in the small town. That's an exaggeration. Obviously there will be many people who come from different backgrounds, beliefs and societal expectations—you want these people to be acquaintances, allies and even friends. At the same time, you should expect to find like-minded people in the town. You should certainly hope to—otherwise you may have picked the wrong town.

It's a common complaint of people who are struggling in their new towns: "There aren't any of our kind of people around." The complaint suggests two responses:

• Could you have predicted this?

• Where are you looking?

If you're a New England prep school graduate moving to a dying coal mining village or a Texas oil magnate moving to a Wisconsin dairy town and you have a fairly limited definition of your kind of people, then you may well not find them. This was one of your tasks in choosing and evaluating the small town and in deciding whether such a move would be right for you. When you approach such decisions with an open, logical mind, you should be able to predict what kinds of people you will find. (On the other hand, if your prediction was wrong, perhaps your best tactic is to admit it and move on.)

Secondly, you're more likely to find certain kinds of people in certain kinds of places. For example:

• Partiers will be at the bar.

• Outdoor people will be outdoors.

• Literary people will be at the bookstore or library.

• People with moral beliefs will be at church.

• Political people will be at meetings.

• Intellectuals will be hanging out at or near the university.

• Career-minded people will be at the office or shop.

It may well be that a town has few intellectuals (and no facilities for higher education) or few outdoors-lovers (and a polluted environment). But before coming to such a conclusion, be sure you've looked for them in the right places. Don't complain about a lack of morals or political beliefs if you've only been frequenting the bar; don't complain about a lack of parties or outdoor recreation if you never leave your office except to go to church.

Finally, if finding a specific brand of people to spend your time with is of particular concern, consider a community planned especially for such people. Private planned communities are created, shaped and marketed to a well-defined niche. If you fit that niche, you may find that being surrounded by like-minded people is the greatest benefit of your new life.

While important, meeting people is by no means easy. If you have moved to a place where you don't know anyone, it will take real effort to get out and meet them. You need to be patient with the process and with yourself. Some days you may not feel up to such work; some days you'll work hard with little reward. But if you keep at it, giving it time and effort, you will be rewarded.

As the saying goes, "There are no strangers, only friends we haven't met." Potential friends are everywhere, as long as you make the effort to form bonds with them. Co-workers, health club patrons, barflies, waitresses, delivery people, neighbors—anyone can become a potential fishing partner, golfing buddy or all-around friend. Initiate an activity and involve them in it. As you become closer to some of them, encourage them to introduce you to others.

But don't wait for others to introduce you. In a large social setting or a small local shop, introduce yourself. As a newcomer, you have a luxury: You're quite certain you haven't met these people before. Introducing yourself is entirely appropriate.

As noted above, it takes patience and hard work; you don't want to be too hard on yourself. At the same time, you want to know when to give up. You may need to give up on yourself: you can't do this, you're too shy, too lonely or you need the bonds of family to help anchor you to surroundings and people. You may need to give up on this town: it's too closed-off, too set in its ways, too different in character from what you're looking for or simply the wrong environment for you. It is as hard to make the decision to leave the town as it is to move there. But achieving a good quality of life often requires numerous hard decisions.

Becoming involved: Bob Renner

"If you step out of your shell and get involved, you will become part of the community," says Bob Renner of Coos Bay, Ore. Bob and his wife, Betty, volunteer at the Coos Art Museum, Shore Acres State Park and their homeowners' association. They have also joined gardening clubs: bonsai, fuchsia and rhododendron. ("My first managerial assignment at Sears was in the garden shop," he says. "It was only a year, but that started a hobby for me. Once you learn the difference between a petunia and a pansy, you're hooked.")

The Renners have also reached out to their neighbors. "If you find reasons to get together," he says, "it works well. Betty had a birthday soon after we moved, so we had a birthday party at a restaurant with six couples from the neighborhood. It would have been unthinkable in the San Francisco area, to ask your immediate neighbors. People here are more available, more trusting, less cynical."

Volunteering has also helped Bob meet interesting people. For example, he notes that soliciting art donations for a museum fund raiser was "doubly rewarding—not only performing a worthwhile public service, but also getting acquainted with members of a stimulating, creative community."

There is some anti-California sentiment. "You don't brag about being from California," Bob says. "Many Californians do live here, and that's pushed the real estate market up. Natives resent that, but it's the harsh reality of the real world." The good news is that although Oregon has a very small minority population, the Renners found very little ethnic prejudice. "Betty is of Japanese descent, though American-born. There aren't many Orientals in the area, but we certainly haven't encountered any problems. If anything, it has opened doors for us!" Bob now serves on the board of the Coos Bay-Choshi (Japan) Sister City Association.

Not everything has been rosy. "There's too much rain to play golf, which I find disappointing," he says. "And we had no expectations of this being a cultural experience, which has unfortunately been borne out. There are many fewer opportunities for foreign cinema, lectures, concerts or sports. Even pro sports on TV—all we get is the network feed."

They've substituted with community activities. "We're in our late 50s, so we're still useful enough to volunteer," he says. "We were looking for a place to kick back and fit in. We found a welcoming neighborhood, a real sense of community. That's exceeded our expectations."

B. Acquiring things

Without question, your new friends and acquaintances will be your most important acquisitions in the small town. In addition, you'll be shopping for a variety of things: staples you've always bought and the accouterments of your new lifestyle. This section contains some hints on acquiring those things.

1. Shopping locally

In all probability, the small town itself will not be able to provide for all of your shopping needs. Most small towns simply don't have the market to support the shops that can provide the variety of specialty and "big-ticket" items you'll need. So your local shopping will probably be augmented by three additional venues:

- Trips to urban areas.

- Catalogs.

- Online, televised and other remote services.

Even the shops and services that exist in town may not be all you want them to be. The local grocery store may have terrible selection and high prices compared to what you're used to. The local bank may have negligible savings account interest rates and high ATM (automated teller machine) fees. Indeed, they may not even *have* an ATM. Though in such very small places, you can cash a $20 check at any establishment in town. Other stores, such as the hardware store and flower shop, may not be open evenings, so you'll have to race home from work to get there by the 6 p.m. closing time. (Note the assumption inherent in that sentence: With an early-morning start and a less-stressful environment, you'll frequently get off work before 6 p.m.)

Meanwhile, the nearby city may have a Wal-Mart, Kmart, Target or other discount store and/or a Costco, Sam's or other warehouse store. These establishments can offer better hours and cheaper prices. However, you should make an effort to shop locally. Only when the local stores can't get what you need or the price differential is in the hundreds of dollars should you abandon the local merchants.

There are several reasons to adopt the "shop locally" philosophy:

- **When you need a gallon of milk, you won't want to drive all the way to Costco.** In addition, the local grocery needs regular patronage—for everything from milk to soup to nuts—to stay in business.

- **The heavier markup on items in the local store usually isn't profit.** Small rural stores have less buying power; they may have paid more wholesale than the warehouse store is charging retail.

- **The higher prices in the local store may reflect higher transportation costs** to get the items there. If you include your time and gas to drive to the city for the same items, you may find little difference in price.

- **The profits from chain stores go to corporate headquarters and stockholders.** The profits from the locally owned store stay local, where they may be reinvested in other local stores (including yours).

- **Nationwide chains typically give employees a poorer deal** than locally owned shops. They offer lower wages, fewer benefits and less loyalty to the employee.

- **Statewide banks typically invest more of their money in big cities.** When you need a loan, the locally owned bank will be more likely to understand the project. They'll offer you a loan where the "big guys" might not—but only if they have the money available from your (and your neighbors') savings account.

The most important reason to shop locally, though, is to support the local merchants. Entrepreneurship, especially in the form of a small family operation, is the source of the American dream—you want to support that, especially when you have a personal connection to the dreamers. What's more, these people's dreams are far more than just making a buck working for themselves. They have the same dream you do: They want to live in this town. They want to take advantage of the same recreation, neighborliness and safety. They believe, as you do, that this experience is worth far more than the higher wages or profits available in the city.

We discussed earlier the fact that the small town is based on community and the city is based on economy—two traits that run counter to each other. Economy—the frenzied search for a better mousetrap and cheaper electronic equipment—creates the vibrancy of the city. Community, on the other hand, creates the safety of the small town. When shopping, you need to acknowledge that and be willing to pay more for those benefits.

2. Shopping for your home

The very first piece of advice that Karen Good of Rockport, Maine, offers people moving to a small town is, "Don't buy. Rent first, for a year or so, to see if you like it. This will also help you decide if you want to live in or out of town and what sort of neighborhood you want."

Buying a home is a major step that includes numerous costs—both financial and emotional. There are the various transaction costs, such as Realtor fees and closing costs; the costs of moving all of your stuff; and the commitment of time and emotion needed to set up your new home. It's a lot to go through if you later decide you really need to move back to the city. It may be easier and wiser to rent first. You might even put all of your stuff in storage and rent a furnished place, or (as I did) furnish it with cheap garage-sale stuff that you can then sell at your own garage sale after your real furniture arrives.

3. The (lack of) importance of shopping

Shopping and the acquisition of "things" are less important in the small town than they are elsewhere. Despite the difficulties outlined here, you may not want to spend too much time shopping, planning to shop or complaining about shopping.

This even holds for the things associated with your new lifestyle. Are you moving to a small logging village because you love wearing flannel or to a fishing village to wear a fisherman's sweater? You don't have to live there to wear their clothes. Of course, weather conditions in such towns frequently require you to wear certain styles of clothing, but there's far more to living in a small community than appropriating its fashion image. If all you want is the image, buy it at your local suburban mall.

Seven tricks for meeting new people

1. **Smash your television.** It's so easy to turn on the TV. Before you know it, you've sat there all night without having any human interaction. If you don't have a TV (or at least don't have cable or a satellite dish), you'll force yourself to go out and participate in activities or hang out in cafes, taverns or coffee houses. For example, if you watch a lot of sports on TV, start doing so at the bar instead of at home. As you become a regular in these activities, you will form bonds.

2. **Cancel your newspaper subscription.** Read the newspaper, but don't do it at home alone. Go to a cafe, order a meal or coffee and read the paper there. Or use the library. Again, you're becoming a regular in a social setting.

3. **Join a health club, aerobics class, basketball league, biking club or similar group exercise activity.** Instead of running or doing calisthenics alone, do it with others.

4. **Go to garage sales.** They are often a social fabric of the town. Ask why they're selling—most aren't moving, they're just getting rid of extra stuff. Examine what's being sold, for two reasons: 1) If you haven't brought furniture, this is a good way to furnish your home (small-town shopping at its finest!). 2) Once you start recognizing things from previous sales, you've shed your "newcomer" status.

5. **Walk around town.** If you live right in town, walk on your errands. Your face will become familiar. If you drive instead, your car will become familiar—but people aren't likely to start a conversation with your car. Meanwhile, it may take them a while to connect your face with your car.

6. **Pay bills in person.** It's easier in a small town—the bank, utility company and other entities to whom you owe money may all be on the same block. In fact, they may even be more convenient than the post office. You'll meet the people who work at these places, as well as other bill-payers, in person.

7. **Let your pet do it.** Walk the dog around town (ideally after the dog's business is taken care of or with a scooper in hand). Your dog will be much less shy than you are about greeting other dogs or people. If and when that happens, you have a ready-made conversation topic.

When you move to a small town, in other words, there's a difference between being a local and some Hollywood version of a local. For example, it's fine to buy cowboy boots and wear them out on Saturday night, but unless you ride a horse, you'll find them otherwise largely useless.

Another shoe example is given by Ted Conover in his book *Whiteout*, an engaging portrait of his move from Denver to Aspen, Colo. He notes that Sorels, the rugged, thick-lined Canadian boots, are "the Aspen winter shoe." But buying Sorels doesn't make you an Aspenite: They have to become gray and worn. "As a pair of Sorels achieves that truly beat-up, utilitarian look, it enters the realm of old Aspen status symbols that help people in their seniority calculations. But if your Sorels still shine, odds are you're (at best) new in town—or, worse, a *tourist*."

Buying boots, water skis, a canoe or a surfboard may be something you're looking forward to. Or it may be something you find you have to do to take advantage of the town's recreational opportunities. But the thrill of acquisition will pass; the steady, solid lifestyle of the small town will remain ever constant.

Chapter 5

Prospering in your small town

How can I survive in this different culture?

The key to small-town prosperity has little to do with money. Sure, you'll need enough to survive on, and without a doubt, economics are the most common reason people give up on a small town to move back to the city. But those who succeed aren't necessarily richer. Instead, they have adjusted their lifestyles, expectations and beliefs to the realities of the small town. They can survive on less money, and they're willing to do so because they have accepted the community and been accepted by it.

In this chapter we'll discuss some of those adjustments—some of the implications of small-town life. Many will probably come naturally to you. Others may challenge some of your deeply held assumptions.

A. Changing expectations

When you visit a foreign culture, you're very aware of differing customs. As a conscientious tourist (or one who wants to fully appreciate the experience of travel), you try to honor and follow them as much as possible. You speak the native language. You learn which common hand gestures are considered obscene. You bow or kneel at appropriate times.

In a small town, though you're still in America and everyone speaks English, there are cultural differences. The etiquette and the outward displays—such as shaking hands—are often the same, but the differences in viewing and responding to the world can run quite deep.

These are some implications and results of the small-town sensibilities we've been discussing throughout the book. While you may have appreciated them on the surface, you may not have thought them fully through. In this section, we'll consistently use the phrase *which means that* to highlight the need to change your expectations.

The small town focuses on abilities, not credentials, *which means that* you need to lose your credentialism. In the city, your circle of acquaintances may have been limited to people of similar professions or similar educational backgrounds. You may have even (subconsciously, perhaps) looked down your nose at others. In a small town, you can't afford to do that. With so few people in town, you can't limit your circle in any way.

Furthermore, there's no need to limit your circle. Often a small-town resident doesn't have a graduate degree (or a college education) because there are fewer opportunities to get one. Going off to graduate school means going away and leaving the town they love to get credentials that place them out of the local job market. It has little or nothing to do with intelligence. In some ways, small-town residents are smarter than you are: They realized years ago that they wanted to live in this town, even if it meant sacrificing "extras," such as additional education. These people may also be quite well-read. If you enjoy literature, you may find some unlikely discussion partners—as long as you don't dismiss them for lack of credentials.

The criterion in the small town is always this: Can you get the job done? It's never: Do you have the credentials to get the job done? Reputation is the credential. A mechanic may not be officially certified by a specific automobile manufacturer but may nevertheless have the aptitude and skills to work on your car. You'll know whether or not he is qualified by his reputation. In a larger community, you may not know a mechanic's customers and so may not be able to judge his reputation—which creates the need for some sort of credential.

The small-town pace is slow, *which means that* you can't be in a hurry. For example, when driving, always stop for pedestrians in the crosswalk. Don't pretend you don't notice them or assume you can make it past before they get to your side of the street. Don't butt into traffic or cut people off. If the car in front of you hasn't noticed that the light has turned green, don't honk in annoyance. When you're waiting at the grocery checkout stand, don't hop back and forth between lines. Choose a line and stick with it, perhaps engaging your neighbor in conversation.

You may have to keep reminding yourself: This is why I moved here. I wanted to get away from the hustling stress of the city. I didn't like being in a hurry all the time, being surrounded by people in a hurry all the time. You wanted that relaxed pace, you got it—day in and day out. Live with it. Enjoy it.

The land is more important to people's livelihoods, *which means that* you have to treat it carefully. Most of the existing rural residents' gripes about newcomers have to do with treatment of the land. For example, if you don't control weeds on your land, they may spread to the adjacent farm. If you don't maintain fences (or if you leave gates open), their livestock (or yours) may wander away. Don't overgraze your property; fully understand local water rights. Finally, be aware that though running free may make your dog happy, it may make your neighbors unhappy. Dogs (even cute, obedient, little dogs) chase live-stock, causing injuries and stress.

You may share your neighbors' interest in land stewardship. But your ignorance can still cause problems—especially if you don't even realize you're ignorant. Seek (and heed) the advice of your neighbors and resources such as a university extension service, Soil Conservation Service or private consultants.

Urban problems don't exist, *which means that* you can be more open, friendly and relaxed. You've adapted your lifestyle to the problems of urban America. But where those problems don't exist, people may see your habits as odd or even unfriendly.

For example, since there are no "undesirables" on the street and no chance of being mugged or approached by a panhandler, people will look at you on the street. They will greet you, if not verbally, then at least with their eyes. Your habits—looking away, looking down, not speaking—may make you appear reserved, off in your own world or superior. People who get to know you will discover that you're not any of those—you're just used to different patterns and perhaps shy and uncomfortable in the new situation. But the rumor mill may see it differently. If people have heard the rumors, it may take them longer to find your good points.

Because there are no burglaries, there's no need for big, fancy security systems. You don't need a car alarm, you don't need an elaborate security system on your house and you especially don't need to light up your lawn like a prison fence. People in small towns strongly resent security systems because they suggest a lack of understanding about what the community stands for. Almost all small towns pride themselves on being safe, open, close to nature and classless. They believe—presumably correctly—that you have moved to town because you too value those qualities. So they wonder:

- If you knew the town was safe and wanted it that way, why would you feel the need for a security system?

- If you knew the town was open and wanted it that way, why would you close yourself off behind your fortified house?

- If you knew the town was close to nature and wanted to take advantage of starry nights and wildlife wandering into your yard, why would you ruin that (for you and your neighbors) with light pollution?

- Worst, if you knew the town was classless (i.e., not focused on material possessions to achieve status), why would you feel the need to own the types of things that require security systems?

You may want the peace of mind that comes from some form of protection. But be unobtrusive about it. Use a security system that will upset only potential burglars, not potential friends.

Because you're not the anonymous statistic of the city, you can't get away with as much. When you lose your temper, it'll be among people you'll see again. If you cheat someone, fail to pay your bill on time or otherwise treat people with less than the respect they deserve, it's far more likely to come back to haunt you. People will recognize your car as the one that cut them off last week; they'll recognize your voice on the telephone as the one that was so difficult when placing the last order; they'll recognize your dog as the one that was running loose in the neighborhood chasing cats. Even if nobody confronts you (in fact, especially so, because when confronted you have a chance to make amends), you may be establishing a reputation. Since reputation is so important in the small town, you want to be sure to get it right from the start.

Popular culture: Twin Peaks

In the television show *Twin Peaks*, an FBI agent probed beneath the surface of a small town in his efforts to solve a brutal murder. *Twin Peaks* gained widespread though short-lived popularity for its endless plot twists and incredibly bizarre characters.

The more Agent Cooper probed, the more it became obvious that the idyllic face of this small town was a complete fake. All of its residents, from the clean-cut sheriff to the disingenuous victim, were hiding secrets such as drugs, extramarital affairs, greed or mental illness. Agent Cooper, the urban transplant who always wore a suit and tie (unlike anyone else in the show or, for that matter, almost anyone in a real small town), was the only force for purity and good.

This was thus a very urban show. Small-town residents didn't recognize any of the story line. Small towns do have their share of problems, including sex, drugs, greed and mental illness. The show, however, presented a community awash in them, its values thoroughly, irretrievably corrupted by them.

Twin Peaks played to urban fears of the small town, including a vicious rumor mill as well as an absurd desire to present a respectable facade. But these small-town fears were mixed with urban fears of violent big cities inappropriately transplanted into the small-town setting.

The bizarre characters were also one-dimensional. Take, for example, the Log Lady, who carried a log around like a pet. We learned little more about her life than this peculiarity. In a real small town, people with strange habits also have conventional habits, and it is because both of them are so widely known that the weirdness can be tolerated.

Twin Peaks was a work of creative genius, expertly realized. But its dark, complicated vision was at odds with the optimism and goodwill that characterize most small towns.

There are fewer people in a small town, so you don't need to mark off your personal space. In the city, surrounded so often by crowds, you get justifiably territorial about your apartment, home or yard. These are the areas where you retreat from the world. In the small town there's more space. Your emotional life may be crowded and your house may not have as many rooms as you'd like, but in terms of geographic area, there's plenty to go around. Because small-town residents place a high value on community, they may be puzzled at your desire to get away from them. As noted earlier in this chapter, this means that the notion of "private" land may be more public than you'd expect. If you own a lot of land, you may want to allow recreational uses, such as hiking, hunting, fishing, swimming, berry-picking, four-wheeling, three-wheeling, biking, cross-country skiing or snowmobiling. You may want to ask users to get your permission first, but be considerate: Don't require a written request, make them call long distance or make them wait a month for a reply.

B. Local perspectives

When you view the world through a small town, you're using a different lens than everyone else. You're seeing a set of perspectives that, though difficult to fully understand until you've been there, you may want to appreciate up front. Understanding these perspectives may be particularly helpful in explaining the behavior of your new neighbors.

1. Rumors

There's no doubt about it: The rumor mill exists. It's a strong force in many small towns. Some people hate this quality of small towns—the fact that everybody always knows what you're doing. Others tolerate or even value it as a byproduct of the intimate community.

Don't expect to have any secrets in the small town. If you tell something to one person, expect that others will find out. Don't be surprised if not just *some* others but *everybody* finds out. You may discover that certain close friends are able to keep secrets—let that come as a pleasant surprise. If you truly have a secret that absolutely nobody should know, then tell absolutely nobody. On the other hand, the fact that you color your hair, you have a ne'er-do-well brother or filed for bankruptcy 10 years ago are everyday secrets whose consequences may not be as bad as you expect. You may find that other people don't judge you as harshly as you do yourself.

The rumor mill is strongest among older folks. Younger, working people have less time to gossip and less need to feel in control of their lives by knowing everything that's going on in the neighborhood. The rumor mill is also strongest in very small communities, where there are fewer potential subjects. Rumors generally circulate most widely about controversial statements or actions. If you punch Fred at the tavern on Friday night, more rumors will spread than if you simply argue with him. Likewise, calling Fred a babbling buffoon will generate more rumors than saying you simply disagree with him about the school bond issue. In each case, the more controversial action prompts people to speculate more about its motives. People also speculate more about things they don't know. If you are close-mouthed about your past, your job or where you got your money, people may try to invent explanations.

Rumors also circulate more about people who are, or seem, absent. When I worked for a software company that moved to a small town, the rumor mill had several far-from-gullible locals convinced that we were making pornographic movies in the basement. Software was a foreign object in this town, exotic enough to sound like a front for less savory activities. But more importantly, all of the employees lived out of town and few made efforts to become part of the local community. The rumors flew because we were foreign and standoffish.

The key to beating the rumor mill is to treat everyone with fairness, kindness and respect. When people know and like you, they'll squelch vicious rumors about you. At worst, they'll come to you for your side of the story.

Of course, treating people with fairness, kindness and respect is something you want to do anyway. One reason you're moving to the small town is that you perceive its residents as being friendly, honest and decent.

Honesty is your most valuable trait. Be forthright; let people know what you're doing and why. If you try to deceive them, shade the truth or hide things from them, rumors will catch up to you. When people don't know all the facts, they'll speculate...and perhaps get it wrong. When they have all the facts but don't believe them, they'll head for the same result. The key, then, is to give people all the facts and not go back on your word.

Several years ago, a large ranch near my town was sold to a Californian with experience in real estate development. When he was interviewed in the local paper, he insisted that he wanted to keep it a working ranch. Nobody believed him. Given the land's development potential, the price he'd paid for it and his background, residents were sure he had something up his sleeve. When he subsequently announced modest and responsible development plans, there was outrage that he had "lied." Since part of the ranch remained in operation, it would be more fair to say he had only stretched the truth, but his lack of forthrightness poisoned his reputation.

Good news spreads, too. We tend to think of gossip as malicious. Indeed, there are certain personality types who unfortunately find a need to say bad things about people. But a third party may also say, "Jeannie seems like a really nice person," or "That company treats its employees well." Since such statements are not malicious, you may not think of them as rumors. But it's the same dynamic at work: people issuing opinions on other members of the community without personal experience.

As noted before, rumors spread in any community. The difference is that in the small town there's just one circle, rather than separate ones for work, church and family. The rumors thus spread more quickly and more comprehensively than you may be used to.

2. Personal knowledge

In a small community, the frame of reference is almost always personal knowledge. Your feelings toward people in the public eye (local "celebrities," if you will) is different because you know them, their families or friends.

You didn't personally know the mayor of Los Angeles, a writer in Detroit or a watercolorist in Orlando. Big-city public figures in politics, sports or the arts are "newsmakers" and you generally know them through the television, newspaper or other media. You may have appreciated the results of their work (an important law, a touchdown, a pretty song) or even shared a particularly strong attachment to place (the law is particularly good for this neighborhood, a folk song captured the flavor of that rally). But you did not have a personal connection with these people.

The media are aware of this lack of connection. They try to make up for it in magazine profiles, with their probing, personal questions, or in tabloids, with their focus on lurid private details. They try to present you with a "true" personality, but it's not the same as true, personal knowledge.

In the small town, on the other hand, you almost always have that personal knowledge. The mayor isn't someone who only runs in political circles; he also sold you your lawnmower. The watercolorist doesn't live in a penthouse apartment in a ritzy neighborhood; she has a rundown shack next to yours. Of course their level of celebrity is different: her watercolors sell for $200, not $2,000; the mayor's job is part time, which is why he's also in the home and garden business. In fact, they are likely not as gifted or skilled in their professions as are the big-city celebrities.

What they do have, though, is a common local perspective. The artist's watercolors accurately capture the beauty of this area: the quality of the light, the brilliance of the flowers. The mayor's campaign platform speaks for the concerns of the townspeople. You thus don't want to dismiss these people. Study and appreciate them, learn from them what's important in this area. Robyn Kratzer of Park City, Utah, says, "There's a public radio talk show that does interviews on issues important to people here. I listen to it to get a sense for the local value system, to hear different politicians and educators. What's important to people? How do they think?"

3. The local newspaper

Small-town papers are a real treat. As you're making the transition from an urban area with all of its problems, you may be quite entertained by what constitutes front-page news in a small town.

You may also be appalled by the paper's journalistic standards or writing quality. Still, you'll want to subscribe to the paper as you're evaluating a town, before you move there and for your first few months (at least) living there. You'll learn a lot about the community.

Of course not all of it will be true. The newspaper may not accurately reflect reality. In fact, no newspaper does. A big-city paper attempts a long-distance view, where a small-town paper, by necessity, is attempting a closeup. This detailed perspective makes the mistakes more obvious.

Additionally, especially with the lower journalistic standards, a lot gets left out. Sometimes this is due to incompetence: not hearing about a story, not having the staff to cover it or not thinking it important. Sometimes it's due to bias: the publisher, editor, sales manager or reporter (or one individual filling all four roles) may have a personal ax to grind or may turn a blind eye to problems with a pet project. Don't believe the paper is an accurate reflection of the news. Be aware of the filters the news has come through and consider how the original source material might have differed. Unless you've been a journalist or a small-town resident, this task can be difficult.

One particular section to beware of is the letters to the editor. Unlike big-city papers, a small-town paper prints every letter it receives. This includes cranks, crackpots and people who have their facts wrong. Do not assume that mean-spiritedness, racism or wrongheaded politics displayed in letters to the editor are representative of the population at large.

The biggest problem with the local newspaper is that usually everybody already knows most of the news. A friend of mine who once worked on a paper in rural Vermont said that the locals read it every week as entertainment to see how many mistakes the reporter had made. They didn't need to read it for informational content because they already knew everything that was going on.

Mistakes at a small-town paper may not necessarily be any greater than those at a larger paper. A big difference, though, is that you didn't *know* the members of the Dallas school committee or the Minneapolis city council or the Atlanta zoning commission. In a small town, they sit next to you at the cafe and tell you what happened at the meeting four days before the paper comes out.

4. Relationships to government

The spirit that fostered the legend of the New England town meeting still exists in many small towns. Government is a participatory process rather than an external monolith.

Many Americans have come to see government as a contractual arrangement, notes Jim Murtaugh, a nonprofit foundation executive who has worked with many small towns. The attitude has become, "I give you my taxes, you give me my services." Yet this is far from the democracy we hope to achieve. Murtaugh says, "I want to imagine that we once were more concerned about creating a just, civil society which recognized that, at a fundamental level, we cannot separate our neighbors' rights and needs from our own without jeopardizing both. I think this view was quite naturally reinforced in small communities and neighborhoods where relationships were personal and where social, political and economic interdependencies were more obvious and valued."

In a small town, then, the democratic ideal is less likely to disintegrate. People have a stronger sense of community and of belonging, which leads to a greater sense of self-government. People are more willing to tackle problems. Furthermore, local government positions are less likely to be full-time professional positions. The tasks are still on a small enough scale that someone can do them as a hobby. "Government," then, is less likely to consist of "bureaucrats and politicians." Instead, on the local level, it's the owner of the print shop, the hairdresser and the mortician who give up their Tuesday nights to help solve community problems. Even outside of New England, where official "town meetings" are rare, community deliberation is much easier to achieve than it is in urban areas.

Given that it's shared by the entire population, government can't be as easily blamed for things. When you complain, "I'm not getting mine," you're viewing government on the contractual level. Conversely, when you say, "What can we do to solve this?" you're using the democratic community approach. Examples of situations that may call for this approach include:

- Snowplowing.
- Sign ordinances.
- Parking regulations.
- Trash collection.
- Parks maintenance.
- Road paving or resurfacing.
- School activities.

Before you storm into the county offices complaining you're not getting enough of these services for the taxes you pay, stop. Take a deep breath. Remember that you're part of the community, and the community solves these problems together.

Village life: Karen Good

"This is not a suburb, it's a village," says Karen Good, who moved from New York City to coastal Maine 25 years ago. "That means it's more integrated. Not racially—rural Maine is fairly homogenous racially—but economically and culturally. Businesses are located next door to houses and there are many different-sized businesses."

The integration extends to social levels as well, she says: "Some people are educated. Some aren't. Some have lived here all their lives and love it. Some are newcomers. Some have lived here all their lives and hate it."

Living in such a village often changes the way you approach politics, Karen says. "Particularly in New England, we have a participatory form of government. You need to understand that you will probably have an active political life. At the same time, you need to be wary of trying to impose your cultural beliefs and lifestyles onto the place you've moved. Watch, see how things work...and then contribute. You need to approach local politics not as one who knows better but as a participant on equal footing with everyone else."

Karen started a business in the small town and has encouraging news for entrepreneurs. "It may be easier than in a metropolitan area because you build relationships. People know you. There are fewer people in the small town but more information about them. We found we could establish credit more easily. This may not still be true, the way credit markets have tightened recently, but it still may be easier in the small town than in the city."

5. Public education

The small town's community focus places a value on educating all of its children. Education is seen as a societal good and an equalizer, providing everyone with at least some basic tools they may need to succeed in life.

If you now live in a metropolitan area, especially if you are a well-educated professional in an upscale neighborhood, your child's education is of utmost importance. Susie needs the best education she can get, you believe, so that she can reach her full potential in life. If you don't feel the public schools are good enough, then you may be willing to spring for a private school.

These are admirable attitudes but in potential conflict with the small-town perspective. First, be sure you're not using a contractual approach to schooling: You pay taxes and Susie gets educated. In a small town, where budgets are tight and there are often fewer demands on parents' time, you may want to volunteer to help run a worthy program. Second, note the way you're placing Susie's individual needs above those of other kids in the community. Isn't it important for *all* of the kids to get a top-notch education? You're suggesting that Susie is more important than Kathy or Jenny down the street. Now, of course you *do* feel that Susie is more important—after all, she's yours. But in moving to the small town you have, in a sense, adopted the entire community.

6. Parochialism

No matter how inconsequential, all small towns put their community at the center of the universe. News is always filtered through the lens of the local perspective. Local newspapers would print the following headline over a small story about the Titanic disaster: "Cruise Liner Sinks; No Locals Aboard." You need to remember that issues that don't affect the immediate community may seem pointless.

No matter how dreary, most small towns think they're the best in the world. You need to be aware that comparisons with your former home may be seen as insults. Until you've established your credentials as someone who loves the town and wants to stay, be wary of praising other places too much.

Consider this situation, which may arise shortly after you move. Someone asks where you're from, you say, "New Orleans," and they respond, "What a great city. I've always loved New Orleans." If you proceed to talk rhapsodically about the wonders of New Orleans, your new friend will wonder why you left and expect you to move back there shortly. If you have only negative things to say about New Orleans, your friend may wonder if you're insulting her positive experiences there or if perhaps you can't say anything nice about a place.

The best answer, as usual, may be to take the active listening approach. Your response could be, "What in particular did you enjoy?" Then you will be able to have a specific conversation about jazz, architecture or beignets without getting bogged down in comparisons.

C. The value of escape

One of the keys to successfully living in a small town is to get out regularly. This may hold true in any situation, but particularly when you live in a small community. You occasionally need to escape the strong personalities, the gossip, the same old routine. When you do so, you will typically come back refreshed and relaxed. Being away will also remind you of the things you take for granted living there, and you'll come back with a renewed appreciation for why you made the move in the first place.

You may want to plan at least one and perhaps two vacations per year. These should be traveling vacations, not vacations where you paint the house, putter around the garden or take advantage of everyday, local recreational opportunities. You may even want to vacation to a city. New York, for example, takes on a real excitement when you visit from a small town. The skyscrapers, the hustle and the diversity of pedestrians make for an exotic experience—completely opposite from your everyday life. As a vacationer, you can stay just long enough to take advantage of the museums, restaurants and shows, while still getting out before you get frustrated with the traffic, crime or cost of living.

You may also want to escape the weather. Small-town people tend to spend more time outside and less time in temperature-controlled offices or automobiles. The weather thus plays a bigger role in your life. You may find it easier to survive a Northern winter by spending a few weeks in a hot Southern climate. You may want to break up a humid Southern summer with a few weeks up North, at the mountains or the shore.

Your escapes to the wider world, however, need not be limited to vacations. You can get beyond the local community in your everyday life using some of the following techniques:

- **Subscribe to magazines.** You will likely find that your daily newspaper does not have as much detail and analysis of the news as you're used to. National magazines may help provide that.

- **Listen to National Public Radio.** NPR provides sophisticated news, classical and jazz programming on stations that are heard in a surprising number of rural areas.

It all comes together on Halloween

In many small towns, Halloween is the biggest holiday of the year. That's quite a statement, considering the family traditions associated with Thanksgiving, the religious atmosphere of Christmas and the patriotism of the Fourth of July. But many people who absolutely, unequivocally love living in a small town say that Halloween is their favorite holiday.

Halloween includes your community "family"; it upholds the celebrants' philosophical values; it's a way of paying respect to the place you live and the principles that place stands for. It thus embodies aspects of all the important holidays, with the added fun of dressing outrageously. It's both a celebration of the small town and an escape from it. It's the social event where the whole town escapes to itself.

The successful small-town Halloween is highlighted by a large social gathering for adults only. Frequently it takes place in a tavern. There's often a live band. And there has to be a costume contest. It's not uncommon for 80 or 90 percent of the party-goers to be in costume.

Many cities, such as San Francisco, are known for their Halloween celebrations, where everyone on the streets is in costume. But there are some fascinating sociological differences between the city and small town.

For one thing, people in a small town work at an elaborate costume not just as a creative outlet, but also for sheer disguise. If you don't cover yourself carefully, you'll be recognized, taking away much of the fun. Some small-town residents will go to the lengths of refusing to speak or speak only with a heavily altered voice to safeguard their deception.

When fully disguised, people are freed of the social expectations and mores of their traditional role in the small town. They can be obnoxious, funny or loud. They can be great dancers or practical jokers. They can invent themselves an entire new personality. In short, they can act as strangers for their friends.

Even if you don't go to such extremes, the presence of people who do makes Halloween all that much more fun. In a city, you can go out and admire the creativity and daring of the wide variety of costumes. In a small town, you have the added challenge of figuring out who's behind the mask. It's always a hot topic, a puzzle to be debated long into the night and often through the following weeks.

> The Halloween experience may not fully click for you the first year, but perhaps by the second or third. Even if you're not comfortable playing a role or wearing a costume, go out on Halloween and savor the atmosphere.
>
> Underneath all those costumes are people just like you. Good, common, decent folk who love the area and the community, who value its security and insularity. Halloween is also the ultimate escape, because you'll be surrounded by people who, to the naked eye, would appear to be utter strangers.

- **Use your telephone.** Expect your bill to go up. You'll want to call your friends back at the place you left or in other locations around the country, if only to temporarily leave town in your mind.

- **Go online.** Get access to the Internet or sign up with an online service, such as CompuServe or America Online. You gain access to discussions, a wealth of information in a variety of forms and even shopping. Remember, however, that going online will cost more in the small town than it does in the city because you'll probably have to pay telephone long-distance charges to the access number.

D. You make a difference

This book has spent a lot of time discussing the character of small towns. We've examined how some attributes of small towns can help or hinder your quest for a better quality of life. But there's no doubt that the most important component of your prosperity in the small town is you. Your character and personality will make the difference in how you adapt to the culture. You will also make a difference in how that small town culture adapts to you and your fellow migrants.

Moving and shaking. People who prosper are movers and shakers. That's a rule in any environment and certainly holds true in the small town as well. On the other hand, movers and shakers are also found in mental institutions. Those unfortunate people didn't move and shake in the same direction as their surroundings.

Becoming accepted: Karen Good

"I'd been warned that people from 'away' don't get accepted," says Karen Good of Rockport, Maine. "But what I found was that if you participate positively—for example, I served on the volunteer ambulance crew—you're no longer functioning as an 'outsider.' And once you no longer think of yourself as an outsider, neither do the people around you.

"But you have to show that level of commitment to be accepted," Karen cautions. "People don't want to bother making friends if you're not going to be there very long. If you're a visitor on vacation 'trying out' this different lifestyle for a year, they won't welcome you into their hearts. And indeed, now that I've been here for a while, I feel the same way: I'm going to reserve my friendship for people who are going to be around long enough to return it."

Karen's first piece of advice to people considering the move is to rent for a year and make sure they like it. But if you're renting, doesn't it look like you're not making a commitment? "I know this seems like a contradiction, but your commitment shows in other ways, such as having your kids in school or trying to build a business. People respond differently to those types of activities."

She has nothing but positive things to say about her move. "I moved here 25 years ago and have never regretted it. Though I grew up in Newark and New York City, moving here was like coming home." Her adjustment period was not all that difficult. "I had to learn about burning wood, how oil furnaces worked and how to keep a garden—skills I need to live here successfully. But on a social level, I certainly found that this is a place full of human beings, just like anywhere else."

To achieve prosperity, you can't be passive. You have to identify what you want and how you can get it from your surroundings. You need to pay attention. Is it possible to get what you want from a given set of surroundings? Is it easy? Will people admire, respect or like you for pursuing such goals, or will they fight, scorn or reject you? If it's the latter, your goals and environment conflict. You'll have to shed one or the other. The American tradition, probably a wise one, is to get a new environment. Rather than trying to change your personality, move to a place where your personality blends in better.

People who prosper devote a lot of energy to their prosperity. Those who prosper financially spend much of their time making or keeping their money. Those who prosper in their marriages or relationships spend time and energy on that aspect of their lives. Those who have prosperous relationships with their communities have been movers and shakers in their friendships and civic responsibilities.

Work. To some, the strategies outlined in this book may seem like a lot of hard work: choose a location, find a job, find friends, fit into the community. But most people won't think of it as work. Meeting new people and forming bonds with them is something most people do instinctively, something many even crave. Doing it all at once, however, is a huge set of new challenges. If you don't like new challenges, be prepared for a lot of "work." If you choose to avoid those challenges and that work, you might as well stay where you are. This commitment also has huge potential benefits. Your personal well-being and quality of life is a cause worthy of a good deal of work and commitment.

Assimilating: Robyn Kratzer

"You can't be a wallflower," says Robyn Kratzer of Park City, Utah about getting to know people. "You have to be willing to get out and meet people. If somebody invites you for a drink, go. Right then, if necessary. I think it's easier with children. The school provides a social structure. You meet people at sporting events or meetings. Especially in Utah, because it's such a family-oriented state. People move here to raise their kids because it's safe.

In addition to understanding the community, Robyn advises paying attention to yourself. "One weekend, Rob [her husband] went to Houston to run a marathon. I made a conscious choice not to follow him. I knew I couldn't run to Houston every time I wanted to do anything. You have to make a commitment: This is your new home and you're going to make it work."

The new home can be larger geographically than the old one. "A saving grace for us has been Salt Lake City, which is quite close. I spent lot of time there at first. It's enough of a city that it gave me a sense of security during the change. I can't picture how someone would adjust moving to a place like Sun Valley, which is three hours from anywhere."

Turning it around. We've been focusing on the advantages (or drawbacks) that moving to a small town will have on your personal life. But the small town is not simply a mirror, something that reflects your image. It is a living, changing organism that can be as affected by you as you are by it.

How will *your* actions change the local community? Consider for a minute the perspectives of other people: How will your presence in town affect their lives? How will it change the social, economic or environmental dynamics of the town? How many people will see these changes as improvements?

The arrival of a big fish can upset the balance of the small pond. Other fish may fear they'll get crowded out. They may fear that the bigger fish will eat their food, foul their playgrounds or swim in the wrong direction. Once one big fish is established, other big fish may invade the pond, upsetting all of the delicate interdependencies of the food web to the point where everything collapses.

A surge of newcomers can have a significant affect on the local community. Often the town is growing because of its amenities—scenery, recreation, culture and history. An influx of self-absorbed newcomers can overwhelm these very amenities. This doesn't mean you shouldn't move to such a town. It does emphatically mean that you need to be aware of and respect local character and traditions.

How do you build and act on this knowledge and respect? Think smart. Think local. Ask about local customs and traditions and why they're important—then follow them. Ask for advice—then listen to it. Ask how you can help—then follow through by providing it.

Appropriate housing. If you're building a house, use appropriate architecture and building materials. You may have always loved adobe, but an adobe house is probably not appropriate for upstate New York. Likewise, a log cabin does not fit the culture and history of a seaside resort.

Use appropriate landscaping as well. If you're moving to an arid or semi-arid area, you can't have the lush green lawn you had in Connecticut. To install one is to deny the unique local character and tradition. It's also environmentally unsound, wasting precious water on plants that simply shouldn't exist in that environment.

Be aware of the effects your house will have on the environment and community. Don't build on top of a ridgeline, where you interrupt everyone's view. Remember that the small town is focused on nature and the attractiveness of the natural habitat, not on the attractiveness of buildings, roads or other manmade structures. Be wary of building on steep hillsides, where you may subject yourself to floods and mudslides and may exacerbate those problems for your downhill neighbors. Don't build in a floodplain or on a barrier island that is regularly washed out by storms.

You'll want to follow these sensible and sensitive practices regardless of laws or existing patterns. The mere fact that there are no zoning regulations prohibiting a practice does not mean it's a good idea. Remember that the small town has long survived on informal community pressure rather than explicitly spelled out regulations. Just because an inappropriate subdivision already exists doesn't mean that you should do the same thing next door (or even buy a house in that inappropriate subdivision). It may well have been constructed by someone who didn't appreciate the rhythms and traditions of the town. You don't want to support such a person financially or philosophically.

Giving back to the community. We've argued that civic involvement will be good for you by helping you meet people and become part of the community. It's also good for your town. By supporting local institutions, you help strengthen the community against the considerable onslaught of modern conveniences.

By becoming involved in the local historical society, you help preserve the area's history. By supporting a theater or arts organization, you help enhance the area's cultural opportunities and provide opportunities for residents to get out and be with their neighbors. By becoming a volunteer firefighter, you help alleviate the risk of fires and help keep taxes low by lessening the need for paid professional firefighters. By joining a service organization, such as the Lions Club, you help with a variety of civic projects. The net result of any and all of these: you improve the way the community functions, which improves its ability to work for you.

Avoiding arrogance. You may have been successful in your career, you may have received a top-notch education, you may have raised a terrific family or been involved in worthwhile causes, but you've never lived in this town. So don't be arrogant. Don't assume you know better than your neighbors how things should be done.

- **Environmentally.** Don't assume you know better than the natives how to treat Mother Nature. Once you have fully researched and appreciated local practices, you may be able to conclude that they're inappropriate. But you don't know that going in.

- **Professionally.** Don't gloat over the fact that you will bring jobs to the area. Just do it, without fanfare. If it's right, if it works, the accolades will come.

- **Politically.** Don't assume that local governments will be happy that you're adding to the tax base. Studies show that in the long run, new residential development eats up far more in services than its residents contribute in revenues. So you're not necessarily doing local governments a favor. By including you in their community, letting you live out this dream, they're certainly doing you a bigger one.

Staying put. The easiest way to become part of a small town is to have been born there...and never leave. You don't really have to *do* a whole lot. When you (and your neighbors) have lived in one place for a long time, you can point to your roots.

The problem comes for those of us who have moved a great deal or whose hometowns have changed beyond recognition. We have no roots. The problem is *not* in recognizing that this rootlessness is a source of unhappiness. (That's easy.) The problem is that we want roots immediately. But you can't transplant roots. You have to stay somewhere long enough to grow them.

When you move to the small town, plan to stay there forever. Even if you know you won't be staying, act like you will. Let your roots grow. *Habits of the Heart* discusses the conflict we all feel between our commitments to our careers and our communities. What if being promoted means moving? How do you make this choice? Some people try to make the choice easier by not becoming committed to their communities. *I'll only be here a few years; it's silly to get involved.* In taking that view, you cheat yourself of the benefits of that involvement.

If you leave town, what will you have contributed? There are few easy ways to answer this question comfortably. If you've had no friends, acquaintances or involvements, then clearly you have not succeeded. If you have brought McDonald's, authentic New York bagels or a film festival, you need to ask yourself if the natives would have chosen such "sophistication" if you had not been there. If you have established an institution (an environmental organization, a festival, an educational program) that doesn't outlast your departure, then your contribution has been as fleeting as your presence.

Oddly, given the current nostalgia for the way small towns used to be, the best answer may be that you simply enhanced what the community already had to offer.

Appreciating what's there. Don't demand from the small town what it doesn't have. Take full advantage of what it offers, but realize that it can't offer everything. Choosing a small town involves tradeoffs. You can't get everything: both the sophistication of the city and the easy lifestyle of the town. If you try to get both, you may just end up with neither.

In *Little Town Blues*, Raye Ringholz writes, "Suddenly the people who moved to Jackson [Wyoming] for its wild scenery, outdoor recreation and frontier flavor started clamoring for paved roads, airport expansion for jet service and increased cultural facilities. Instead of fitting into frontier life themselves, they tried to impose upon their new home the gentrification of the places they had left. Polarization of the community resulted."

Though I am a newcomer myself, I tend to agree with Ringholz in blaming the newcomers for polarizing small towns. One could say change was inevitable and blame the old-timers for refusing to go along, but the fact remains that the newcomers came to Jackson because they liked the society the old-timers had created. (And one can substitute any number of small towns all around the country for Jackson, though few provide such vivid contrasts.) It thus doesn't make sense for them to immediately start tearing down that culture by insisting on the amenities of the places from which they came.

I can't blame someone for liking "civilization," whether that means paved roads, jets or dozens of varieties of pasta in the supermarket. What I *do* blame them for is expecting they can "civilize" a community without changing it. Or expecting that those changes will be all good. In terms of the community's values—which, whatever they were, must have been a big part of what attracted you in the first place—such wholesale changes brought on by outsiders are destined to be mostly bad.

Again, the point is not that people can't move to small towns. It's that any newcomer needs to respect what already exists and work for change within those traditions and values.

Chapter 6

Preserving your quality of life

How can I keep the magic alive?

The quality of life you seek is embodied in the word "community." To preserve that quality of life, you will need to preserve the sense of community.

Community performs five social functions, according to sociologist Roland Warren:

- Producing and distributing goods and services.
- Transmitting values.
- Enforcing norms and values.
- Facilitating social participation.
- Assuring mutual support.

These are all basic societal needs. When we condemn our community as having failed us, we are saying these needs have gone unmet.

Communities need not be geographic. They can arise around work (consider professional associations), hobbies (such as model trains, quilting or Harley-Davidson motorcycles) or religious affiliations (members of a church may be dispersed throughout a town). Additionally, technology is creating new forms for community, such as online discussion groups.

Are these new forms making geographic communities irrelevant? It's unlikely. Consider 30 years ago, when company towns and idealistic communes generated excitement. Many proved short-lived; they failed to provide some of the basic societal needs, such as facilitating social participation or enforcing norms and values. The yearning for community so many Americans currently feel suggests that none of these alternatives has been able to serve as a complete substitute.

However, simple geographic proximity is not enough. The lack of community spirit in many cities proves this. So does the existence of "lifestyle enclaves," to coin a phrase by Bellah and colleagues in *Habits of the Heart*. Simply playing bridge together, sharing a hedge between yards or exchanging pleasantries during a church social does not create the deep bonds of community.

A true community replicates society on a smaller scale. We often see community as a collective identity. As Richard Sennett said, a community is "strangers whose lives touch." Yet the community is also our source of strength in achieving our individual goals. "Becoming one's own person, while always a risky, demanding effort, takes place in a community loyal to shared ideals of what makes life worth living," Bellah and colleagues write.

Pat Jobes—the sociologist who found that four out of five migrants to Gallatin County, Mont., left before five years were up—declared that this area was not a true community. Residents of the area, he said, had no sustained, personal, informal commitment to other residents. (In a vicious cycle, newer migrants may have been discouraged by that lack of a sense of community and moved away.)

Community, then, is not some external force. It is not some commodity that can be purchased at a store or rated on a scale of one to 100 in a book. Communities that succeed do so because of their members' commitment to the group. In a successful community, you feel that you belong and that the group is an extension of yourself. The opposite applies as well: The group feels that each member belongs, and each member is an extension of the group. These conditions can only arise when members of the group have shared enough—struggles, experiences, background or difficulties—to trust each other.

By no means is a small town the only geographic setting in which you can achieve a sense of community. It can grow in urban or suburban neighborhoods, rich or poor neighborhoods (though perhaps a mixture of incomes is most desirable), historic or brand-new neighborhoods. What it takes is people willing to make that commitment and make it seem worthwhile to everyone else.

In fact, if you're a person who cares about community, you may be of better benefit to society by *not* moving to a small town but instead creating that sense of community right where you are. Rather than starting your life over in some small town, reform and reshape the place you now live to fit these dreams. After all, you already have family, historical and/or economic ties there; you can simply add this piece to your puzzle.

Furthermore, by no means does a sense of community provide all the answers in life. For example, one of the major struggles of modern life is dealing with diversity. How do we relate to people who are different from us? We idealize the small town (and picture an idealized small town) where everyone shares our ethnic, religious or socioeconomic background. But in doing so, we set up the same problem of "outsiderism" that we decry in too-rigid small towns. When a community excludes people based on geographic, ethnic, religious or socioeconomic background, then it isn't living up to our standards. If America is to be a true melting pot, we can't set up such divisions. We must come to terms with diversity. Most small towns are of little help here.

In a broader sense, the ideal of the small town simply does not give us the tools, resources or mindset to look at society on a larger scale. The slogan "Think globally, act locally" is actually quite difficult to achieve simultaneously. Many forces in the larger society threaten this small-town ideal we so cherish.

There's packaged entertainment, which can replace conversation, and musical recordings, which can replace front-porch jam sessions. There's the importance of a career, which can replace roots to a place. There's the unfortunate xenophobia provoked by our country's ever-increasing diversity, which replaces the open friendliness that a well-functioning community uses to greet outsiders. There's the pell-mell of development, which can replace historical or environmental features with condos and mini-malls. Perhaps most dangerously, there's our culture's penchant for isolationism, which (though it's beneficial in small doses) could replace most of our human interactions with a "society" of individuals each trapped in a technological fortress.

Of course nobody can stop all of these forces—nor would anyone necessarily want to. But keeping them at bay and preserving that sense of community is something all of us can do. Long after you've moved to the small town—or even if you never do—turn off the television one night and host a pot-luck dinner party. Turn down a promotion or a project at work because it would intrude on the rest of your life. Sit on your front stoop and wave at people walking by. Ask an old-timer to tell some stories of your neighborhood's history. Take a chance on your fellow citizens, hoping that a conversation will be as entertaining, sustaining and useful as anything the technological wizards can dream up. Be a part of your community, and it will become a part of you.

Appendix

Resources

This appendix lists resources—books, organizations or ideas—that may be of help as you contemplate moving to a small town. The appendix is broken into four sections. The first three sections roughly correspond to chapters in the book:

- Deciding if you want to move.

- Choosing and evaluating a small town.

- Finding a job.

The fourth section covers miscellaneous other resources.

A. Resources to decide if you want to move

Your decision to move is based on your personal attitudes, beliefs, philosophies and values. It's something only you can know. Thus, the resources in this section are simply tools to help you clarify your thinking—they won't do the thinking for you.

A **counselor** may help you clarify your feelings about such a move. The counselor may ask penetrating questions about what it is you really want and whether a small town can help you achieve those objectives. Get recommendations on counselors from your pastor or doctor. If you're not interested in getting professional counseling, be sure to talk over the issue with **friends and family**. They know you well; if they're smart and honest, you may find their opinions useful.

Concerned about your finances? Make up a **budget**. How much will you need to live on? How much house can you afford? Sometimes these questions can only be answered by penciling out some alternatives. You may need the assistance of a professional financial planner.

At least one national **newsletter** provides advice "to people serious about moving to the country." *Sticks*, which is quoted in this book, is available for $36 a year by calling 800-639-1099 or writing Route 1, Box 1234, Grafton, NH 03240. Publisher Lisa Rogak takes Master-Card and Visa.

Several **books** offer advice on moving to a small town:

Betsy and Hubbard Cobb, *City People's Guide to Country Living*, Macmillan, New York, 1973. Though it's more than 20 years out of print, much of the advice in this book is surprisingly appropriate.

Lisa Rogak, *Moving to the Country Once and for All*, Country Roads Press, Grafton, N.H., 1995. Tips from the editor of the newsletter *Sticks*. To order, call 800-639-1099.

Marilyn and Tom Ross, *Country Bound! Trade Your Business Suit Blues for Blue Jean Dreams*, Communication Creativity, Buena Vista, Colo., 1992. Tips on moving out of the city and starting a business in the country. At times too chatty, at times irrelevant, but at times extremely useful.

There are also dozens of books about people's experiences moving to small towns. Some of my recent favorites include:

Rick Bass, *Winter: Notes from Montana*, Houghton Mifflin, Boston, 1991. A naturalist from the South moves to a remote Montana ranch. Bass' writing style is literary yet wonderfully approachable.

Ted Conover, *Whiteout: Lost in Aspen*, Random House, New York, 1991. An insightful journalist and cabdriver profiles what may be the trendiest small town in America.

Anne Tyler, *Ladder of Years*, Alfred A. Knopf, New York, 1995. A novel in which the protagonist starts a brand-new life in a tiny Delaware town where she doesn't know a soul. It rings true.

Many **movies and television shows** depict contemporary small-town life. Though idealized, some can provide valuable insights to what your life might be like. Those mentioned in this book's sidebars include the movies *Groundhog Day* and *The Englishman Who Went Up a Hill but Came Down a Mountain;* the television shows *Cheers, Twin Peaks* and *Northern Exposure* (all off the air but perhaps shown in re-runs); and the public radio show *A Prairie Home Companion* (broadcast in most areas on late Saturday afternoons).

Your most trusted source may be the **personal touch**. Do you have friends or family who have moved to a small town? Call them and learn about their lives. Share your goals and ask their opinions. Be sure to talk to people you know who tried living in a small town and didn't like it. They may offer experience as valuable as anyone.

Finally, you should **visit** small towns. There's absolutely no substitute for personal experience. Planning a sales trip? Detour for a few days to check out nearby small towns. As you get more serious, you might even invite your family along. Planning a vacation? Find a small town offering the vacation amenity you're looking for. Make sure it's a "real" town and not a community constructed solely for the resort. (For example, as enjoyable as it is, Walt Disney World's "Main Street USA" is hardly a legitimate picture of what your life would be like in a small town.) If you enjoy it, be sure to go back in the off-season.

B. Resources to choose and evaluate a small town

1. Choosing a small town

If you want to leave the city but have no idea where to go, use these resources to help you identify potential candidates.

Where is your **family**? Family members can provide an anchor to your new life as well as introductions to your new neighbors. Moving to a long-time family home can also provide you with a sense of spiritual rootedness.

Where are your **friends**? Friends can serve as a surrogate family; they also presumably share some of your interests. If you and Jerry used to golf together all the time, Jerry's new home may be near a great golf course.

What areas have **you** enjoyed? Have you traveled a lot on vacations or business? Which areas have you found attractive?

You may also want to check out **books**. A popular mini-industry rates places to live using a variety of categories.

Eric and Margaret Burnette, *My Kind of Town: An Essential Guide to Finding the Ideal Place to Live*, Chronicle, San Francisco, 1995. This guides you through the processes of narrowing the search to the best town for you.

Norman Crampton, *The 100 Best Small Towns in America*, Prentice Hall, New York, 1993. Crampton's profiles of these 100 towns are outstanding. However, if you don't already have an idea of where you want to move, the book has little advice to help you select a town.

Lester J. Giese, et. al. *The 99 Best Residential and Recreational Communities in America*, John Wiley and Sons, New York, 1992. This covers strictly private planned communities.

Lee and Saralee Rosenberg, *50 Fabulous Places to Raise Your Family*, Career Press, Franklin Lakes, N.J., 1993. Though some of the fabulous places are larger than small towns, the Rosenbergs evaluate them with a clearheaded approach to improving your quality of life.

Lee and Saralee Rosenberg, *50 Fabulous Places to Retire in America*, Career Press, Franklin Lakes, N.J., 1994. This offers the "fabulous places" approach for retirement communities.

David Savageau and Richard Boyer, *Places Rated Almanac*, Prentice Hall Travel, New York, 1993. The authors rate metropolitan areas, not small towns, but their exhaustive, reasoned approach may help you think about how to evaluate a small town.

David Savageau, *Retirement Places Rated*, Prentice Hall Travel, New York, 1994. This offers the "places rated" approach for retirement communities.

G. Scott Thomas, *Where to Make Money*, Prometheus Books, Buffalo, 1993. This rates only metropolitan areas, but some may appreciate its focus on economic opportunities.

G. Scott Thomas, *The Rating Guide to Life in America's Small Cities*, Prometheus Books, Buffalo, 1990. This covers "micropolitan" areas: cities of at least 15,000 population that are outside of traditional metropolitan areas. Chock full of statistical rankings, the book may appeal more to ratings buffs than to people looking for advice on moving.

PHH Technology Services (800-210-8852) offers a **software package** based on the book *Places Rated Almanac* (again, it covers metropolitan areas, not small towns). Along similar lines, *Money* magazine has a **World Wide Web** site (http://pathfinder.com/money) associated with its annual rating guide issue.

Do you enjoy maps? Then maybe you want to spend time with an **atlas**, judging towns by their locations. The *Rand McNally Commercial Atlas and Marketing Guide* (updated annually and available at your library) contains a wealth of demographic and economic statistics as well as detailed maps of every state in the nation.

Do you enjoy statistics? Then consider three publications of the **U.S. Census Bureau**: *The Statistical Abstract of the United States, The State and Metropolitan Area Data Book* and the *1990 Census of Population and Housing*. You may want to approach these tomes with specific questions in mind so the task doesn't seem too overwhelming.

Do you want your destination to have certain recreational amenities or fulfill your hobbies in certain ways? Then check out the national **association** for your hobby or activity. Is there a local chapter of your professional society? Is there an accredited practitioner in a given field? Is there a sanctioned league for your sport? An association directory or staff person may be able to answer such questions. If you don't know the name or address of an association, check out the *Encyclopedia of Associations* (Gale Research, Detroit, updated annually) available at your local library.

Also be sure to check out **magazines** for your hobby, interest or region of the country. Whether it's golf, tennis, backpacking or bowhunting, there's a magazine for aficionados. Most states also have regional magazines. To find magazine names and addresses, check out the *Directory of Publications and Broadcast Media* (Gale Research, updated annually) at your library.

Magazines may also have feature articles on specific towns or resorts. They may rate outstanding facilities, such as top golf courses. They may even have articles geared specifically toward people like you who are considering moving. Beware of articles rating the "Top 10 Undiscovered" towns of any stripe. Despite its inherent stupidity, this is a favorite topic of magazine editors. Needless to say, after the thousands of people who read the article invade the town, it will not be "undiscovered" any more.

2. Evaluating a small town

Once you have one or several candidates, you'll want to evaluate each one to see if it fits what you're looking for. To do so, use the following resources.

Get a **chamber of commerce packet**. Almost every chamber has a packet of materials it sends to prospective residents. Some have special packets for retirees or entrepreneurs, so be sure to ask. If you ask for materials and they don't arrive, ask again—sometimes chambers are staffed with volunteers who are stronger on enthusiasm than organization. To find addresses and phone numbers, use directory assistance or the national chamber of commerce directory, which should be available at your local chamber.

The packet should include many of the following materials. If it doesn't, you may want to pursue them on your own:

- Real estate guide.

- Phone book.

- Church directory.

- Economic and demographic information on the town.

- List of chamber members.

Subscribe to the local **newspaper**. To get the address and phone number (if it's not available in the chamber packet), look in the *Directory of Publications and Broadcast Media* (Gale Research, updated annually). If the town has more than one publication, you might want to check out all of them. Circulars, shoppers, and arts, human-interest or "alternative" publications can tell you a great deal about the town.

Do a **literature search** on the town and area. Perhaps someone has profiled the town in a book or magazine article. Maybe they've even written about moving there! Reading about that town's history may also help you learn a lot about its character.

Request information about the local **hospital**. Does it provide emergency services? How many full-time physicians are there in town? Any specialists? Is there a nearby regional medical center? How is the hospital's financial status—any danger of it going out of business?

Use the chamber materials, yellow pages and other sources to find out about local restaurants and culture. Are there minor league or college sporting events? Is there a restaurant with your favorite dish or ethnic specialty? If there's a local arts, theater or musical organization, write to get a list of local events it sponsors and/or the benefits of membership.

To learn about the **weather**, watch TV's *The Weather Channel* or follow the national weather map in your local newspaper. (Some papers don't give detailed enough treatment to national weather patterns. If in doubt, check out the famed four-color map in *USA Today*.) For general weather information, you can also look in *Climates of the States* (Gale Research, 1985).

Check with your favorite **airlines** to see how close they fly to your destination. How convenient are the connections? Do they use jets or props? How stable is the service? Is it often affected by weather? If one carrier stops serving the airport, are there viable alternatives?

City or county governments or the chamber may have **land-use** and/or **economic development plans**. If you're familiar with these types of documents, be sure to get hold of one.

Again, however, your best source of information will be personal observation. **Visit!** Use your eyes, ears and nose. Do you like the view? Is the architecture pleasing? Do you like the quiet or the sound of the wind? Does it smell "clean" or "industrial" (or polluted)? Check out specifics: How's the selection in the grocery store, video store and/or bookstore? What movies have been playing recently? What cultural or recreational events are going on this weekend? Go to as many places and events as you can. Do you like the band playing at the local tavern? Do you like the services at a local church? Do you like the local beach or golf course?

The most important research of your visit, however, is in generalities rather than specifics. Do people seem friendly? Do they seem happy? Do you feel happy? Do you feel comfortable? Can you picture yourself walking or driving around this area as a resident? Does this community feel like it could be home to you?

C. Resources to find a job

If moving to a small town involves a career change, you may want to see a **career counselor** because:

- Your current career would not be available in the small town.

- You want to adapt your current career to telecommuting or consulting.

- You want to get out of this career and into something better.

Get recommendations from your pastor or your company's personnel department.

You may also get valuable information from the following books:

Richard Nelson Bolles, *What Color Is Your Parachute?* Ten Speed Press, Berkeley, Calif., updated almost annually.

Jerry Germer, *Country Careers: Successful Ways to Live & Work in the Country*, John Wiley and Sons, New York, 1993. Some useful (if pricey) discussions of the economic aspects of the move.

Joyce Lain Kennedy, *Hook Up, Get Hired: The Internet Job Search Revolution*, John Wiley and Sons, New York, 1995. Using computer hookups to find employment.

Marsha Sinetar, *Do What You Love, the Money Will Follow*, Paulist Press, Mahwah, N.J., 1987.

The Internet and other **computer networks** have discussion groups about moving to a small town and finding jobs remotely. On the Internet, you might check out the Usenet groups misc.rural, biz. jobs.offered, misc.jobs.offered, or misc.entrepreneurs. On CompuServe, visit the Working at Home and the Retirement Living forums. The World Wide Web also has several employment search options.

If you're considering starting a business, be sure to check out regional **economic and demographic data**. Is the regional market big enough to support you? Is it growing or shrinking? Ask the chamber of commerce or state department of commerce about resources that can help you find and evaluate such information. (Demographic data may also help you decide if the town has an acceptable number of people in your age, ethnic or educational bracket.) You may also want to find out what **other start-up businesses** exist and how successful they have been.

D. Other resources

What is the role that community plays (or increasingly fails to play) in contemporary American life? How is that tied to the places we live? You can work toward your own answers to these questions with help from books including:

Robert Bellah et. al., *Habits of the Heart*, University of California Press, 1985. A very readable analysis of contemporary American sociology with worthwhile and useful recommendations on using community to make your life more meaningful.

Joel Garreau, *Edge City*, Doubleday, New York, 1991. A fascinating account of the rising mall-and-office-park culture, including some powerful arguments why these "edge cities," rather than small towns, may be the preferred home of the future. Garreau's previous book, *The Nine Nations of North America* (Houghton Mifflin, Boston, 1981) is an excellent if somewhat outdated guide to regional differences.

Kenneth Jackson, *Crabgrass Frontier*, Oxford University Press, New York, 1985. A history of suburbia, containing insights on how the American character affects our living patterns.

Daniel Kemmis, *Community and the Politics of Place*, University of Oklahoma Press, 1991. An impressive argument that a focus on place can improve people's citizenship and thus improve democracy.

Editors of Time-Life Books, *The Community*, Time-Life Books, New York, 1976. Though outdated, this book is an accessible introduction to the theories sociologists have about community.

Some other interesting books include:

Ron Powers, *Far from Home: Life and Loss in Two American Towns*, Random House, New York, 1991. An eloquent book arguing that small towns are threatened by both poverty and affluence. People are leaving for better opportunities while others are arriving for weekend or second-home tourism.

Luther Propst et. al., *Creating Successful Communities: A Guidebook to Growth Management Strategies*, Island Press, Covelo, Calif., 1990. How to avoid polarization and help your new community deal effectively with change. At press time, Propst was completing a new book, tentatively titled *Gateway Communities*, with photographer Robert Glenn Ketchum.

Robert Reich, *The Work of Nations*, Alfred A. Knopf, New York, 1991. An interesting discussion of the implications of the "new global economy."

Raye Ringholz, *Little Town Blues: Voices from the Changing West*, Peregrine Smith Books, Salt Lake City, 1992. A lucid, heartfelt account of the struggles of some growing small towns in the Rockies.

Michael Weiss, *The Clustering of America*, Harper & Row, New York, 1988. Uses the ZIP-code analysis of marketing firms to break the nation into 40 neighborhood types (or clusters). It's heavy (and fascinating) on analysis, though not necessarily useful in helping you find or evaluate a small town.

You may want to put a **conservation easement** on a large property in a rural area. For more information, contact the Land Trust Alliance, 1319 "F" Street NW, Suite 501, Washington, DC 20004-1106; 202-638-4725.

Index